Secrets for Success

SECRETS FOR SUCCESS

—Failure is Only a Comma Not a Full Stop

By

Prof. M.S. Rao

Corporate Trainer in
Leadership Development & Soft Skills

UNIVERSITY SCIENCE PRESS

(An Imprint of Laxmi Publications Pvt. Ltd.)

BANGALORE • CHENNAI • COCHIN • GUWAHATI • HYDERABAD
JALANDHAR • KOLKATA • LUCKNOW • MUMBAI • RANCHI
NEW DELHI

Published by :

UNIVERSITY SCIENCE PRESS

(An Imprint of Laxmi Publications Pvt. Ltd.)
113, Golden House, Daryaganj,
New Delhi-110002

Phone : 011-43 53 25 00
Fax : 011-43 53 25 28

www.laxmipublications.com
info@laxmipublications.com

First Edition : 2011

OFFICES

✆ **Bangalore**	080-26 61 15 61	✆ **Chennai**	044-24 34 47 26
✆ **Cochin**	0484-237 70 04, 405 13 03	✆ **Guwahati**	0361-254 36 69, 251 38 81
✆ **Hyderabad**	040-24 65 23 33	✆ **Jalandhar**	0181-222 12 72
✆ **Kolkata**	033-22 27 43 84	✆ **Lucknow**	0522-220 95 78
✆ **Mumbai**	022-24 91 54 15, 24 92 78 69	✆ **Ranchi**	0651-221 47 64

USS-9532-100-SECRETS FOR SUCCESS-RAO **C. 1706 /010/06**

Typesetted at : Shubham Composer, N. Delhi.

Dedication

Dedicated to my wife, Padmavathy who has stood by me through thick and thin. She is the source of strength and spirit in my struggle for survival and success. She sacrificed her personal time in support of this book.

To my elder son, Ganesh Sai and younger son, Ramakrishna Sayee for their valuable inputs and proofreading the manuscript.

CONTENTS

FOREWORD

It has often been said that to be a successful person you must study other successful people and learn to think like they think and do what they do. Many of us have asked ourselves, "What does it take to be a successful leader or business leader" and you will often find topics and discussions focusing around goal setting, self affirmations, dreaming big.

Don't worry about the "how" to accomplish your goals but "what" goals do you want to accomplish. The "how" will appear when the conscious and subconscious work together.

Prof. M.S. Rao has written a wonderful book which offers great insight and sage advice on how to become successful. The advice to students is very timely about looking for opportunities. **Prof. M.S. Rao** goes on to advise them not to look at lack of success as a failure but as a way of teaching us to look for another answer.

The importance of goal setting is clear for it has been said, a written goal is an achieved goal. This book provides you with a clear roadmap on how to be successful. This book will provide you with the secrets for success.

Lenny Laskowski

International Professional Speaker

National Best Selling Author, *10 Days to More Confident Public Speaking*.

PREFACE

The future belongs to those who believe in the beauty of their dreams.—Eleanor

Welcome to the book titled **'Secrets for Success'**.

Purpose of the Text:

Success is the sweetest word in the world as everyone would like to achieve. But very few people can only achieve. What are the reasons behind it? What are the common qualities and traits required to achieve success is still a mystery. What makes people to succeed? Is it only the hard work or something else behind success? Is there any formula for success? In fact, there are several qualities and traits that are essential for success. To name a few are self-confidence, self-esteem, self-awareness, self-discipline, self-motivation, self-determination, self-control etc.,

Success means many things for many people. For a college student, success means scoring good marks. For a businessperson, success means making more profits. For an unmarried person, success means having a good spouse. For some people, success means getting recognized by others in the society.

Success is different from achievement. Accomplishing anything that is intended is considered an achievement. In contrast, success means recognition from others. Succinctly, success may be personal progress, professional advancement and social development. Everyone wants to taste success in life. But no one knows exactly what makes people tick. In this context, it is essential to find out the secrets for success.

Features of the Book:

This book is divided into seven chapters. The first chapter is a prelude to the secrets for success. It defines success and provides you the formula for achieving success. It outlines the example of Richards who compromised his passion to become a trainer for the sake of his survival by joining as manager. As a result, he could not perform well. It differentiates between strength and courage. It focuses on building positive, right and strong attitude. It touches on eleven essential E's for developing better personality. It concludes with the author's vision of India by 2020.

The second chapter outlines *'Traits for Your Success'*. It dwells at length about traits and tools for self-improvement such as self-awareness, self-esteem, self-confidence, self-discipline, self-determination, self-motivation and self-control. It defines punctuality, explains the advantages of punctuality and outlines the tips to be punctual. It summarizes that punctuality pays to succeed in your life.

In the succeeding chapter titled *'Strategies for Your Success'* you will discover the leader within you. It helps in uncorking your hidden potential. There is a lot of significance attached to affirmations because it is the first step to roll out your strategies for success. You will get to know how to dream and think big. There are several myths and truths associated with hypnotism. It describes the methodology of hypnotizing your mind for success. It states synchronizing both conscious and subconscious mind. It describes Mahatma Gandhi adopting non-violence and truth for achieving India's independence as an out-of-the-box approach. In this 21st century the illiterates are the ones who don't unlearn, learn and relearn. It concludes with goal setting from the perspective of Indian students.

In chapter four titled *'Secrets for Your Success'*, developing killer instinct, building teams, practicing humility and developing networking skills are highlighted. It lists out certain skills which are commonly essential for everyone for personal, professional and social success. It focuses on NLP (Neuro-Linguistic Programming) which helps in better communication and personality. It emphasizes on communication skills and body language. It sums up with various facets of mentoring for career advancement.

The chapter five captioned *'Tools for Your Success'* sets the ball rolling to brand yourself to stand out from the pack. It provides tips for health and wealth. You can assess your behaviour style and personality type through MBTI (Myers-Briggs Type Indicator). It helps in making right decisions, managing your mind and enhancing your memory. It emphasizes that solitude is fortitude. You learn to cope up with your failures and overcome from depression. It outlines the causes, effects and remedies for anger. Balancing work and personal life is a tough task. It offers tools for better work-life balance. Finally the chapter concludes with the knack of giving and receiving feedback.

The penultimate chapter titled *'Success for Students'* relates success from the perspective of students. It brilliantly relates between parents and children, teachers and students and root and fruit. It highlights SWOT (Strengths, Weaknesses, Opportunities and Threats) analysis both individually and institutionally. It unfolds the importance of study and note taking skills for students. The chapter concludes that students should learn lessons from their failures and should write a resume of failures for enhancing their success rate at the corporate world.

The concluding chapter compares eagles with leaders. Knowledge management is widely talked about across the world. It conveys message that there is pleasure in sharing knowledge for the benefit of mankind. It reveals that 'Knowledge, Attitude, Skills and Habits (KASH)' is the king but not the cash as people think. It highlights Peter Drucker's concept of knowledge workers who are going to lead the world. Only thing constant in this world is change. Therefore you need to reinvent yourself constantly. It appeals to the readers that character and career should not be kept in somebody's hands. You need to stick to your convictions and pursue your passions with perseverance and persistence to excel in life. At the end of the book, the author appeals the readers emotionally with a clarion call, **'Failure is only a comma, not a full stop'.**

Besides, the book contains key terms, brain storming exercises and activities at the end of each chapter for evaluation and practice.

I am confident that this book helps you in reaching your tipping point.

—Author

1

INTRODUCTION

Success is a journey, not a destination. - Ben Sweetland.

LEARNING OBJECTIVES

After reading this chapter and doing the exercises, you should be able to:

- Know the meaning of success.
- Write the formula for your success.
- Understand passion and how it contributes to your success.
- Differentiate between courage and strength.
- Build positive, right and strong attitude.
- Comprehend the thought process of below average, average and above average individuals.
- Develop better personality for achieving success.
- Dream India by 2020.

CHAPTER OUTLINE

1. What is success?
2. What is the formula for success?
3. Passion, survival and success
4. Love, courage and strength
5. What is your attitude?
6. Individuals, issues and ideas
7. Personality development
8. India-2020

WHAT IS SUCCESS?

People create their own success by learning what they need to learn and then by practicing it until they become proficient at it. - Brian Tracy

The seven letter word that everyone is attracted to achieve is 'success'. Success means many things for many people. For a college student, success means scoring good marks. For a businessperson, success means making more profits. For an unmarried person, success means having a good spouse. For some people, success means getting recognized by others in the society. Accomplishing anything that is intended is considered an achievement. In some cases achievement is synonymous with success. To put it succinctly, success may be personal development, professional growth and social status. Everyone wants to have success in life. But no one knows exactly what makes people tick. It is in this context, it is essential to find out what is the formula for success.

WHAT IS THE FORMULA FOR SUCCESS?

Formula for success: Under promise and overachieve. - Tom Peters

Success is the sweetest word that excites all of us. But everyone cannot reach it. Only a few can reach it. Why is it so? Is there any magic wand for the successful people?

Success is the confluence of several ingredients such as passion, vision, mission, execution and feedback. Whenever you want to achieve something in your life, you must know what you love the most-passion. Passion is like fire brewing in the heart and if tapped becomes an inferno. Passion is closely connected to more of heart than mind. It is more of chemistry than physics. Passion does not settle for less. It craves for more. It doesn't let you sleep. It keeps you on toes. It makes you restless. It excites you. It is a typical scenario where it makes you highly focused and task oriented.

Passion

The key that unlocks energy is desire. It's also the key to a long and interesting life. If we expect to create any drive, any real force within ourselves, we have to get excited. - Earl Nightingale

Passion is an immense love towards one's area of interest. It is a fire that keeps the people moving forward. It is immeasurable and intangible and it can only be felt, when one achieves success. It never listens to 'No' and always listens to 'Yes'. It makes the people to go any extent to achieve anything under the sun in the earth. The fact that many inventions occurred and the human civilization prospered and evolved to the current stage is because of the passion.

Passion keeps the people focused. It never distracts from the cherished goals. It keeps the people in the right track and in the fast track. No amount of criticism hinders the passionate person.

Passion is nothing but the burning desire to become big. Passion is like a volcano hidden among the people. It keeps burning internally and drives the people ahead. It is the passion that led Dhirubhai Ambani to build Reliance Empire in India. It is the passion that led Gordon Binder to turnaround Amgen Company. These passionate leaders had clarity and knew where they were going.

Don't ape other successful people blindly as it ends up in a fiasco. What clicks others may not click you. What is required is to find out what touches your heart the most. What are the areas of interest that drives you and gives you kick for moving ahead? Most of the people successful in the world are basically passionate in what they did. They did what excited them. They did what brought joy while doing. They tapped their inner talents. They discovered their hidden strengths. They carried forward their raw abilities ruthlessly.

Vision

A person without a goal is like a ship without a rudder. - Denis Waitley

The second successive ingredient for success is vision. It clearly tells you where to go in your life. It reminds your present status in life. It directs you in a specific direction based on your passion. Most of the successful people are visionaries. They know what they want where they want to go in their lives. They set their directions properly and move ahead successfully. Succinctly, it is like placing the ladder on the right side of the wall.

Mission

Spectacular achievement is always preceded by unspectacular preparation. - Robert H. Schuller

The third ingredient for achieving success is mission. It tells you how to go. Once the direction has been set, the mission unveils the methods, tools and techniques involved in following a specific direction. It reminds of the resources that are essential for following your path to success. It is at this journey the constant efforts and energies are essential to move toward success. It is necessary to equip the skills and abilities for achieving towards. In brief, it is like climbing the ladder.

Execution

Thinking is easy, acting is difficult, and to put one's thoughts into action is the most difficult thing in the world. - Johann Wolfgang von Goethe

The fourth ingredient towards success is execution. It is the toughest task. It is easier said than done. There will be number of practical bottlenecks that hinder the path to success. There are both internal and external forces and factors contribute towards execution. The internal factors can be easily managed as things are very much within human control. Self-discipline, self-motivation, hard work, perseverance, determination and grit will play a crucial role. The external environmental factors which are beyond human control may disturb the path to success. A few call the same as fate. It can either make or break you as a successful person. People who have high internal locus of control don't believe in destiny. These people strongly feel that their destiny is in their hands. They try to control the external environment as far as possible. If they are not able to manage and face setbacks during the process, they pursue their execution with more energy and enthusiasm. The difference between the successful and unsuccessful people is only effective execution. It will tip the scale towards success.

Feedback

If you can't fly, run!

If you can't run, walk!

If you can't walk, crawl!

But whatever you do, keep moving towards your goal........ -Martin Luther

The last ingredient for achieving success is taking feedback. It is a review process where you look at how far you reached your goals and objectives. If you failed to reach why did you fail? How to overcome the failures and what remedial measures can be taken to pursue the path towards success. Feedback helps in aligning your efforts effectively towards your goals and objectives. Confucius aptly put it, "When it is obvious that the goals cannot be reached, don't adjust the goals, adjust the action steps."

Takeaways

Don't lower your expectations to meet your performance. Raise your level of performance to meet your expectations. Expect the best of yourself, and then do what is necessary to make it a reality. - Ralph Marston

The road to success is not a cakewalk. It requires lot of struggles and sacrifices. To sum up, you need to be passionate in whatever you undertake. You have to set out your goals and objectives which becomes vision. You set out a clear path or roadmap towards your success and that is known as mission. Mere words won't pay you but deeds play a crucial role for ensuring success which is execution. Finally, it is equally necessary to take stock of the situation periodically for remedial and correction action which is known as feedback. When all these ingredients are effectively integrated success would touch your toes.

A Warrior Doesn't Give Up What He Loves... He Finds the Love In What He Does. - Socrates

PASSION, SURVIVAL AND SUCCESS

Richards was passionate in becoming a trainer. His ambition was to become a successful trainer in leadership. He faced several lows and highs in life throughout his life. Having come to the middle age, he decided to make use of his corporate experience by becoming a successful trainer in leadership. Although he tried for several jobs for becoming a trainer he failed to become. He had several employment offers other than trainer. Since he had family with children he had several responsibilities. Therefore, he decided to compromise with his passion and joined in a multinational organization as middle level manager. He was able to deliver the goods on an average basis but could not utilize his full potential. For him, survival became more important than his passion to become a trainer.

Likewise, we find many people compromising with their passionate areas and settling down for less than what they aspire, desire and deserve. Can the Richards' decision be justified? Can he grow in the current job that he does for the sake of survival? It is a debatable issue.

Life

Life is replete with complexity and unpredictability. Anything can happen at any time and many things are out of our control. A few people struggle to control the external factors and achieve success. And a few people compromise with what they can do with in the internal factors and survive. Everyone's life revolves around these three factors like passion, survival and success.

Success

Success comes when there is confluence between one's expectations and realities. Success can be defined as the result arising when there is matching between dreams and desired outcome. It comes when the right person is in the right place at the right time. Success comes when the forces and factors in the internal and external environment are effectively managed and coordinated.

People cannot achieve when they compare with others. You can achieve success when your performance is superseded or surpassed by previous performance. For instance, initially if you run 15 kilometers in one hour and subsequently if you run 16 kilometers within the same time, it means you are successful. Never compare yourself with others as it leads to frustration. Everyone is unique. No two individual are alike. Even twins are not alike in temperaments. How can you compare with others?

Takeaways

Passion is the key to success. Find out where your heart is. Tap and channel your energies and efforts in those areas. Do what you love to do. Fear not for failures. Fear not for criticism. Look at your goal. Hit the bulls' eye. Only then, you can achieve success in your life.

Loving what you do is survival. Doing what you love is success. Pursuing what you desire is passion.

LOVE, COURAGE AND STRENGTH

Being deeply loved by someone gives you strength, while loving someone deeply gives you courage. - Tao Tzu

When you love someone you will have courage to go to any extent. When someone loves you it gives you strength because there is someone to take care of you. That makes the difference between courage and strength. Besides, it is the strength that ensures your survival and it is the courage that ensures your success. It is a blessing when someone loves you deeply. However it is a blessing for the other person when you love.

Love is like a perennial river flowing without any let up. It is a kind of feeling and emotion implanted among the people. It involves emotions, feelings, desires, and attitudes. It need not to be a physical attraction. Love brings smile and happiness. Love enhances interpersonal relations and commitments. Pure love removes negative thoughts from mind.

Love has nothing to do with age. Love can blossom at any age. It is all about igniting your spark. When some people see someone, the spark gets ignited and it is nothing but love. When you love someone with pure heart you can definitely win the love. Even if the loved ones are separated, they get connected after some years if the love is pure and strong.

We rarely find anybody dying for the sake of brother, mother and father. But we find people dying for the sake of love. Why it is so? Courage comes from love. When your loved one is being taken away or is hurt you get courage to go to any extent to protect even risking your life.

WHAT IS YOUR ATTITUDE?

Whenever you're in conflict with someone, there is one factor that can make the difference between damaging your relationship and deepening it. That factor is attitude. - Bentley, Timothy

What is Attitude?

Attitude is all about how you think and present yourself to others. If you think positive, you get positive results and if you think negative, you get negative results. Whatever you want you will get, provided you have the right attitude. It is a mindset that takes you to tool set and skill set to be successful in your endeavors. Attitude is like your antenna. You can receive right signals only when your antenna is correctly placed.

Positive, Right and Strong Attitude

Attitude is a little thing that makes a big difference. - Winston Churchill

To be successful, you need to have not only positive attitude but also right attitude and strong attitude. For instance, mere thinking to become an engineer may not fulfill your desire to become an engineer. You need to put in your efforts and energies in a right way which calls for right attitude. If students copy during examinations they may either be caught red handed or may come out with success. But such success will not last long. If the attitude is right it leads to putting in the efforts in a right way thereby getting the right results. Finally, mere positive and right attitude may not give the desired results. What is needed is the strong attitude to pursue whatever you want till the end. Hence, it is desirable to have positive attitude, right attitude and strong attitude to be successful in your own area of interest.

Diana as a Marketing Executive

The greatest discovery of our generation is that human beings can alter their lives by altering their attitudes of mind. As you think, so shall you be. - William James

Diana was an introvert and socially inept woman by nature. She did MBA in the domain of marketing. But marketing requires a separate skill set such as being extrovert, social, talkative and emotionally intelligent. She joined as a marketing executive in a multinational company where she had to constantly interact with her colleagues and also with her customers. She had to be social, talkative and extrovert. Initially she had lot of difficulties as her nature was not compatible with her professional duties. Gradually she changed herself to be successful so as to stay in the job and evolved as a successful marketing executive. How could she evolve as a successful marketing executive? It is basically because she changed her attitude as per her job profile and became successful. We need to change ourselves to be successful in the world with the changing times and it is possible only by changing our attitude.

Advantages of Attitude

Our attitudes control our lives. Attitudes are a secret power working twenty-four hours a day, for good or bad. It is of paramount importance that we know how to harness and control this great force. - Blandi Tom

It is the attitude that can bring hundred percent results in our lives. Attitude helps in enhancing our aptitude. Positive attitude helps in facing several challenges in our day to day life. It makes us competent and confident. It changes our perceptions about adversities. It minimizes conflicts and maximizes peace and tranquility. Attitude converts an ordinary individual as an extraordinary individual. It increases the productivity and performance at the workplace.

How to Build Your Attitude?

Where the loser saw barriers, the winner saw hurdles. - Robert Brault

Positive, right and strong attitude can be built by deleting unwanted files from our minds. Our minds are cluttered with lot of unwanted information and data. We need to gradually remove the unwanted items and replace it with the areas of our interest.

Stay with positive and healthy people who will feed you with positive thoughts, ideas and information. It helps in filling your minds with positive attitude. Start the day with a positive note so that the entire day goes positively. When things are not favorable try to accept the realities, be flexible and mould yourself as per the situation with a right attitude.

Positive Vs Negative Attitude

When one door of happiness closes, another opens; but often we look so long at the closed door that we do not see the one which has been opened for us. - Helen Keller

We can show our importance by helping not by harming people. It all depends on our attitude. For instance, if a doctor thinks of showing importance by saving the life of a patient then doctor has positive attitude. On the contrary, if the doctor thinks of showing importance by causing the death of a patient, it indicates negative attitude. If an engineer thinks of showing importance by building a great structure or dam, the engineer has a positive attitude. In contrast, if the engineer thinks of showing significance by collapsing then it is a negative attitude. Similarly, if a teacher shows importance by teaching and grooming a student then the teacher can win the hearts of the student through positive attitude. On the other hand, if the teacher shows importance by brow-beating or bullying the student it demonstrates a negative attitude. To put in succinctly a person with positive attitude always thinks of helping and winning. In contrast, a person with negative attitude always thinks of harming and defeating others.

Takeaways

Life is 10 percent what you make it and 90 percent how you take it. - Berlin, Irving

The common thread running across all successful people in the world is positive, right and strong attitude. It makes them rise above the rest. It makes the world to sit up and take notice. It differentiates between leaders and followers. Therefore, have a positive, right and strong attitude to grow personally, professionally and socially as a successful person as well as to bring difference in the lives of the people.

INDIVIDUALS, ISSUES AND IDEAS

If you have an apple and I have an apple and we exchange these apples then you and I will still each have one apple. But if you have an idea and I have an idea and we exchange these ideas, then each of us will have two ideas.- George Bernard Shaw

All individuals can be judged by the way they maintain their friend circle. A below average individual always talks of other individuals whether it is good or bad. An average individual always discusses about the events, issues, activities and problems. And finally, the above average individual always focuses on ideas and solutions. All individuals are alike but their thought processes are unique.

The individuals who are above average and who always crave for solutions and ideas are sure to succeed in their lives. Besides, these individual are always out of their comfort zone thus switching over to effective zone. If they feel that the effective zone becomes the comfort zone they switch over to the next higher orbit. They never remain silent and they are always passionate about challenges and changes.

PERSONALITY DEVELOPMENT

Everyone thinks of changing the world. But no one thinks of changing himself. —Tolstoy.

Personality development is a cluster of various traits such as attitude, aptitude, ability, awareness, character, courage, confidence, creativity, logical thinking and analysis, reasoning abilities, sense of humor, self analysis, self-motivation, self-discipline and self-confidence. There is a no clear cut definition related to the concept of personality development. To put it precisely, it is a combination and confluence of various virtues and traits that enable a person, to survive, sustain and succeed in his personal, professional and social life.

Communication skill is one of the major traits that influence the success of any individual. These days, lot of stress is laid on this skill as it is a sure shot to success in the corporate world. Communication skill consists of both verbal and non verbal language. One can communicate effectively and efficiently by carefully articulating both verbal and non verbal language.

Eleven Essential Es

There are 11 essential Es everyone needs to be equipped with for better personality development such as Energy, Enthusiasm, Expertise, Emotional Intelligence, Endurance, Edge, Excellence, Example, Empathy, Effectiveness and Enterprise. Everyone needs to posses higher levels of energy both mentally as well as physically. There should be a strong enthusiasm towards the chosen area of interest. Effective interest in field will make individuals as the master of their trade or field thereby crowning them with third E - Expertise. It will make them rise from the rest. Fourthly, it is the Emotional Intelligence which is all about being mentally and emotionally balanced. It also includes the ability to get along well with others effectively and efficiently. It is also known as people skills.

The fifth E is the Endurance. It is the ability to sustain the setbacks and shocks in one's life. It also includes anticipating and expecting problems and being unmoved and undeterred by any kind of the threats arising out of external forces and factors. The sixth is the Edge. It is nothing but the ability to take extreme unfavorable and unpleasant decisions even though it causes displeasure and discomfort. It is rightly said, "If going gets tough the tough gets going". It is also about being ahead of others.

The seventh E is Excellence. It is the ability to put efforts to give best without looking for perfection. It is very clear that perfection is not the yardstick one should strive for. And it is very difficult to measure the perfection perfectly.

The eighth E is Example. There is a need to set personal example and motivate and inspire others. For instance, Mahatma Gandhi practiced what he preached thereby setting as a personal example for his followers to emulate. He mixed and moved with common people and understood their problems and acted according to the pulse of the people.

The ninth E is the Empathy. It is always essential to empathize with people. It is necessary to listen properly and patiently to the problems of the people by stepping into their shoes. Without empathy it is very difficult to understand and arrive at the clear cut solutions.

The tenth E is Effectiveness. It is quite opposite to efficiency. An effective person does right things and an efficient person does things rightly. Effective individuals believe in putting qualitative rather quantitative efforts. They are smart at optimum utilization of resources and have uncanny ability to deliver their best despite having several constraints.

And last but not the least is the ultimate eleventh E - Enterprise. These individuals are dynamic, fast and risk takers. They come forward to experiment new things and are unmindful of failures. They learn from their failures. They love adventures and have daring and dashing attitude.

All the above eleven elements are essential for the development of a successful personality. The human mind has vast hidden potential and man uses only 10 per cent of the potential and the rest 90 per cent remaining untapped. Those who recognize this fact can unlock and uncork their hidden potential and transform themselves from ordinary individuals to extraordinary individuals.

Talents and Skills

All individuals are born with talents. Talents are inborn whereas the skills are honed by reading, observation, practice, training and experience. Talents are god gifted and the skills are man made. Usually a successful personality is a combination of 20 per cent nature and 80 per cent nurture. If 20 per cent is innate, then the rest 80 per cent can be developed by triggering the inborn talents. Unless there is an earnest effort to realize and tap the talents then it is very difficult to develop the same. Several leaders have become great as they realized their talents and channeled their energies constructively, creatively, productively and fruitfully.

Reading number of books will enlighten and provide new ideas and information that will pave the way for creation of new concepts and models. Reading the biographies and autobiographies of successful leaders across the globe broadens the mental faculties and enhances imagination levels. Right attitude, adequate skills and proper knowledge will lead to higher confidence levels.

Decision vs. Destiny

The decision determines the destiny. It is, in fact, the positive thoughts that will result into noble actions. The actions over a period of time become habits. The healthy habits in turn will lead to positive attitude. It is like looking at the things positively. This again gives rise to aptitude which is nothing but having a specific bent of mind and inclination towards an area of activity. The character is strongly built on the aptitude of the individual. And the ultimate destiny depends on the credentials of a strong character. It has been rightly said, "You sow an action, you reap a habit. You show a habit, you reap a character. You sow a character, you reap a destiny".

Comfort Zone vs Effective Zone

Motivational guru Zig Zigler Zig said, "97 per cent of the people live in comfort zone and 3 per cent of the people live in effective zone". It is very difficult for any individual to come out of his comfort zone as there is no element of risk is involved in this zone. It is only a few successful individuals who live continuously in effective zone and grow and evolve themselves as leaders. And they continuously shift from one orbit to another orbit once they are convinced that their effective zone becomes a comfort zone over a period of time.

Positive Attitude

The globe has become smaller due to the rapid growing technology. People should cultivate the positive attitude towards other people without parochialism. Love your mother but do not hate others' mother. Love your religion, region, language, culture, community but do not develop hatred towards others'. Everyone has a place to live in this world. Let us learn to respect others' cultures and values then only you can expect reciprocal response from others.

Education and Character

One must acquire wisdom to attain knowledge and one should acquire knowledge to attain a good personality. Ideas and ideals are powerful determining factors in the progress of a personality. Confidence and optimism are the two tools that would promote personality development. At the same time, good character and right education are the two sides of the same coin and one without the other has no meaning to a purposeful and productive life. So the secret to success lies in proper personality development. A little push in the right direction can make a big difference.

INDIA - 2020

A developed India by 2020 or even earlier, is not a dream. It need not be a mere vision in the minds of many Indians. It is a mission we can all take up - and succeed. - A P J Abdul Kalam.

Indian civilization is one of the oldest one in the world and we are proud to have cultural richness and India was one of the richest countries in the past. Gradually many changes have taken place and especially with the Portuguese being strong at navigation, they discovered sea routes to various countries and they set up their colonies. Subsequently, French, and finally British set up their colonies all over the world after the Industrial revolution. When they departed India, they fully plundered our wealth and left India in a financial mess.

Ever since independence, India saw many upheavals because British left India with many geographical complications and implications. As a result, we had to face wars with Pakistan in 1948, 1965 and 1971. And also India faced the onslaught of Chinese incursion in 1962. All these things led to many social, economic and political problems. Besides, the policy of mixed economy adopted by Pundit Nehru did not pay off. It has been since early nineties the Indian economy began looking up due to the liberalization, privatization and globalization initiated under the leadership of late P.V.Narasimha Rao when he became the Prime Minister. All these economic policies and reforms paved the way for rapid growth of our country and the world began taking India seriously. In addition, there is a talk of India emerging as an economic Super Power in the near future. In this context, let us evaluate India's potential by conducting SWOT Analysis.

SWOT Analysis of India

Strengths

India, with a population of 1.1 billion and a middle class that is larger than the entire population of US, is one of the world's largest untapped markets. - Satveer Chaudhary, Senator, Minnesota.

Below are the few competitive advantages India has:

- About 16 per cent of the world population lives in India.
- Gateway to international markets in SAARC countries.

- Well developed research and development (R&D) infrastructure.
- Largest resources of untapped natural resources.
- World's largest democracy.
- Information technology base, in terms of both software and hardware.
- Technical and marketing expertise.
- English as the preferred business language.
- A vibrant capital market with 25 stock exchanges with over 9,000 listed companies.
- The largest supplier of cost-effective technical and non-technical manpower.
- Conducive environment for foreign investments by providing freedom of entry, investments, location, choice of technology and import/exports.
- A well-organized judicial system with a hierarchy of courts.
- Legal protection for intellectual property rights.
- A transparent approach for promoting domestic and foreign investment.
- Declining share of agriculture and allied industries in the GDP. The Economic Survey 2000–01 reveals that the contribution of services sector to the GDP is 40 per cent whereas agriculture and industry contribute 30 per cent.
- Increased investments in the priority and high growth sectors such as software, electronics, food processing, oil and gas, power, electronics and telecommunications, chemicals, electrical equipment, food processing etc.,
- A well organized banking system with a network of 63,000 branches supported by a number of national and state-level financial institutions.
- Offers a large market (middle class population of over 25 to 35 crore with increasing purchasing power).
- Current account convertibility and capital account convertibility for foreign investors.
- Increase in the number of joint ventures or wholly-owned subsidiaries most of the domestic companies consolidated around their area of core competence by typing up with foreign companies to acquire new technologies, management expertise and access to foreign markets.
- Deregulation of interest rates with a greater freedom to banks to assess credit requirements.
- Large and solid infrastructure throughout the country.
- Simplified systems for administration in government departments.
- Special investment and tax incentives for exports and certain sectors such as power, electronics and software.
- Lower tariffs for trade.
- A transparent approach for promoting domestic and foreign investment.
- Significantly large manufacturing capabilities through latest technologies.
- India's growth is really productivity-led, rather than investment-led.

Currently India is a nuclear power and is openly exhibiting its intentions to play a key role at the global level. India has her own brand image across the world. It is different and unique in many ways from the rest of the countries in the world. We survived many shocks and setbacks because of resilience.

Weaknesses

We have disputes with both China and Pakistan which are yet to be resolved. When British left India, they left many of the border disputes unaddressed. And the onus now lies with India to resolve the same. Because of the unresolved long pending border disputes with Pakistan and China most of our energies and efforts are focused in fighting the issues rather than concentrating on the developmental activities. No nation can develop as long as it has problems with its neighbors.

We have bureaucratic bottlenecks and widely prevalent corruption which hinders the progress and development. Lack of capital is another impediment for rapid growth. Unfortunately we have cross border terrorism arising out of unemployment opportunities. The present slowing GDP growth and increasing inflation is matter of grave concern.

At times cultural differences, linguistic barriers and regional imbalances among various regions led to infighting among the people and it has become a big stumbling block for progress. Due to the unemployment the youth take to guns thereby giving rise to terrorism. Although we have huge natural resources we have rarely exploited the same. Lack of opportunities at the domestic front led the skilled precious human resources to leave our country and work abroad thereby leading to Operation Brain Drain.

Opportunities

You can't cross the sea merely by standing and staring at the water. — quoted Guru Dev Rabindra Nath Tagore.

India is the second largest populated country in the world and sooner or later will dominate the world in population. We need to convert quantitative human resources into qualitative one. Presently India has the affluent middle class — estimated at over 20 crores or equivalent to the entire population of Indonesia. Research reveals that by 2020 we can have more than 60 per cent of the people in the middle class who will have disposable incomes. Currently India's consumption rate is 64 per cent of GDP and mostly it is services driven growth. When the consumption levels go up there will be more demand for production and more employment opportunities for us. There will be rotation in business leading to circulation of money. Therefore, there will be opportunities for the rapid growth of our economy. Presently many foreign companies have set up their shops due to the rising population and rising disposable incomes. Sensing the opportunities many foreign MNCs are entering India for reaping the economic benefits. It is in this context, Arun Sarin, ex-CEO Vodafone said, "India is on a roll and we are happy to be rolling with India".

The Indian companies after the introduction of the New Economic Policy shed from the protectionist attitude and started competing with their counterparts. Currently we find many Indian MNCs who are in a shopping spree to acquire foreign companies. Tata group acquired many foreign companies be it in steel segment, tea, or chemical or in automobiles. So is the case of Ambani and other business houses in India.

Research reveals that one per cent of India has been crossing the poverty line each year for the last 25 years. And that adds up — 200 million Indians have crossed the poverty line in 25 years. Slowly and steadily many Indians will cross the poverty line and thereby minimizing the percentage of poverty.

Threats

By 2011 the government expects half of India's population to be living in the cities. The urban poverty is posing a major threat than the rural poverty. The rural poor have some space for life and some how they can survive but the urban poor are the worst hit thereby posing a danger for the society and the economy.

Although Indian economy is growing rapidly it is solely dependent on American economy. If America catches cold India sneezes and that is the plight of India economy today. Presently the Indian economy is picking up well but due to American recession the Indian economy is being affected badly. Therefore, it is essential to insulate Indian economy from American economy.

When we glance at internal environment like strengths and weaknesses it is very obvious that strengths outweigh weaknesses and similarly when we look at external environment like opportunities and threats it is crystal clear that opportunities outnumber threats.

India vs China

India is a long term bet with stability . . . China is a short term bet with volatility. — said Stefan Krause, Head of Sales and Marketing - BMW AG.

According to the available reports four countries will have bright prospects in the near future which are abbreviated as BRIC – Brazil, Russia, India and China. Both India and China are competing with each other with the latter having better economic edge currently.

Presently India's working population is approximately 40 crores and that of China's is 80 crores. But in 2025 the roles will be reversed with India having 80 crores working population while that of China having 40 crores. It is basically because China's aging population problems and the democratic dividend that we talk about vis-à-vis India. Presently, half of the India's population is under 20 years of age. Noted global management guru CK Prahlad also envisioned about a strong economic India by 2020.

It was David Crystal who said that the "language of the world at the end of the 19th century was British English; end of 20th century was American English. And he predicts that it will be Indian English at the end of the 21st century". In the case of China, they have total disadvantage as they don't know English and they are trying to learn now.

India has a very strong IT base and however, it would grow at 18 per cent which is second to China where the latter would grow at 20 percent, according to the market research firm Forrester and that becomes a great challenge for Indian IT sector.

India has many constraints and it could grow economically with in the democratic framework where as in China there is communist set up. In this context, it can also be said that India has law and China has order.

Areas to Address

We have lot of waste land that needs to be allocated to the landless poor so that they can cultivate and earn their livelihood. If every family is allotted with a piece of land and provided with water and power facilities the land gets developed as well as the people make their living and they get engaged in a right direction.

Even after six decades of independence we are not in a position to provide compulsory primary education to all. Efforts may be made to see that children aged between 6 to 14 years are encouraged to go to schools as it eliminates child labor also.

Focusing on environmental issues is also equally important. We have to cut carbons and the corporates should be taught to be friendly with ecology and the development should be ecology driven. There is a need to resort to afforestation to check ecological imbalance.

Ours is basically an agrarian society and a gradual shift to services sectors is essential. Focusing on infrastructure is the need of the hour. Unless we have strong infrastructure we can not afford to have strong superstructure.

Cultivate the mind set of *'what we gave to the nation not what nation gave to us'* as it makes us more accountable and responsible. The Indian media is more banking on negative information rather than on positive one in order to ensure their struggle for survival and also to take on their rivals in their segment. It is an unhealthy trend. If they focus on positivism and resort to constructive criticism then they can enlighten the society with right knowledge and information and also they can succeed in the long run.

There is need for political reforms to make our democratic process more meaningful and qualitative. Criminalization of politics should be checked. Politicians with criminal records should not be allowed to the legislatures and parliament. Harmonious balance amongst the four pillars of democracy — legislature, executive, judiciary and press is vital. It should be made mandatory that politicians should have basic education for contesting in elections. No person should occupy the higher offices of President and Prime Minister at the centre and Governor and Chief Minister at the states more than two times.

Militarily we need to strengthen our forces by allocating adequate budget for defence so that we can be prepared to meet any eventualities as we have threat from both China and Pakistan. Resolving the border disputes with both the countries through diplomatic means is to be accorded priority.

CONCLUSION

The best way to predict the future is to create it. — Peter F. Drucker.

As every individual likes to grow, similarly every country likes to grow. It all depends on the mindset of the people. Cultivating a right mindset is the need of the hour. We can learn a few lessons from the V formation of the birds that conveys certain qualities and characteristics.

When birds fly they get into V shape and start their journey. By forming into V shape the birds minimize the drag and maximize the speed thereby enhancing the speed of journey by 71 per cent. During the course of journey they shift their roles and responsibilities. If any one of the birds is hurt or hit by gun shot or falls sick, a few birds will escort the sick bird or the wounded bird to the ground and extend all kind of support to bring the bird to normalcy and then they restart their journey with other group of birds by V formation. If the bird is not able to revive the escorting birds wait till the death of the bird and then they resume their journey. From this V formation of birds we can cultivate the qualities like team spirit, unity of direction and command, sense of belongingness, common goal and objective, fraternity and leadership. All Indians need to cultivate these qualities and characteristics to grow as strong individuals as well as to build a strong India.

MESSAGE

It is the nature of man to rise to greatness if greatness is expected of him. — John Steinbeck.

India is set to become a politically mature, economically vibrant, socially stable, culturally rich and militarily strong country with in a short span if the present trend persists. Our former President, Dr.A.P.J. Abdul Kalam has a vision that by 2020 India will become a developed country.

When small countries can lead why India cannot with a population of billion plus lead? Let us not only make managers but also leaders who can motivate and inspire passion among the people. Presently Indians are leaving for overseas for better pastures and the day is not far away where foreigners will come and work in our country.

Let us have fire and passion to make India a great nation. The youth have to be trained, groomed and guided in a proper direction by channeling their energies and efforts in a right perspective. Providing right education and character and stressing on ethical values can tip the scales in favor a vibrant nation. Let us benchmark with the best in the world. Let us dare to dream big, think big and achieve big. Everyone should note that to aim low is a crime.

The author is confident and bullish that India will become a developed nation much before 2020. And also he strongly believes that we will lead the leaders of the developed countries as a Super Power by 2050.

The dream is not what you see in sleep. Dream is the thing which does not let you sleep. — JAI HIND

KEY TERMS

- Success
- Vision
- Execution
- Attitude
- India - 2020
- Passion
- Mission
- Feedback
- SWOT analysis

BRAINSTORMING EXERCISES

- What do you mean by success? Write briefly your own definition of success.
- Write you own formula of success.
- What do you mean by passion? Is passion required to succeed in life?
- Is it justified to sacrifice your passion for the sake of survival?
- What is the difference between strength and courage?
- How can you build better personality?
- Briefly explain the difference between attitude and aptitude.
- What is the difference between positive attitude and right attitude?
- What do you mean by comfort zone?
- Briefly explain Eleven E's. Check yourself how many Es do you have. How can you relate these with success?
- What do you mean by talents and skills and what is the difference between the both?
- Write your own SWOT analysis of India.
- Write your vision of India 2020

ACTIVITY

What gives your 100 per cent success?

Answer: ATTITUDE. When you count the numerical position of the letters of the word 'attitude' from alphabet and add the numbers, then you get the total as 100. For instance, the value of A is 1, the value of T is 20, the value of I is 9, the value of U is 21, the value of D is 4 and the value of E is 5. When you sum all these numbers you get 100. Therefore, it is the 'attitude' that gives you 100 per cent success.

REFERENCES

Author's Blog: <http://profmsr.blogspot.com/>

2

Traits for Your Success

The toughest thing about success is that you've got to keep on being a success. Talent is only a starting point in this business. You've got to keep on working that talent. Someday I'll reach for it and it won't be there.

LEARNING OBJECTIVES

After reading this chapter and doing the exercises, you should be able to:

- Understand traits and tools for self-improvement.
- Have awareness about yourself.
- Appreciate causes, effects and strategies to build self-esteem.
- Build your self-confidence.
- Inculcate self-discipline.
- Realise significance of self-determination.
- Know the secrets of self-motivation.
- Understand sutras for self-control.
- Maintain punctuality.

CHAPTER OUTLINE

1. Self-improvement
2. Self-awareness
3. Self-esteem
4. Self-confidence
5. Self-discipline
6. Self-determination
7. Self-motivation
8. Self-control
9. Punctuality

SELF-IMPROVEMENT

There's only one corner of the universe you can be certain of improving, and that's your own self. - Aldous Huxley

There are several ingredients for improving yourself. A few of them are; life long continuous learning, passion towards chosen areas of interest, thinking round the clock with positive affirmations, coming out of comfort zone, attitude of gratitude, helping others, networking, etc., Before we look at the ways and means of self-improvement, let us know what is all about self-improvement succinctly.

What is Self-Improvement?

Perfection does not exist - you can always do better and you can always grow. - Les Brown

Self-improvement is also known as self-help where in individuals are keen to bring out behavioral changes for their betterment. It may be physical, economical, intellectual and ethical. Everybody desires to achieve success in chosen areas. Success is possible though sustained self-improvement.

There are several thinkers and writers who pioneered self-improvement through their books. The author, Dale Carnegie (1888-1955) published the book titled *'How to Win Friends and Influence People'* in 1936. He had several failures in his career and wrote the book which is a run away hit. Another author, James Allen published a book titled *'As a Man Thinketh'* in 1902 which depicts that whatever the way individuals think they become be it positive or negative. Napoleon Hill is yet another author who published a book captioned *'Think and Grow Rich'* in 1937 which mentions that thinking rich will make individuals wealthy and prosperous. Besides, several authors and thinkers contributed in the domain of self-improvement thereby rising a ray of hope for others especially for those who are under depression.

Tools for Self-Improvement

Unless you try to do something beyond what you have mastered, you will never grow. - C.R. Lawton

- Open up your mind and heart. Always be flexible and receptive to learning.
- Develop positive affirmations. Inking rather than thinking positive affirmations will deliver better results. Lee Iacocca aptly quoted, "The discipline of writing something down is the first step toward making it happen."
- Set realistic goals and objectives.
- Manage your time effectively.
- Take continuous feedback.
- Explore your strengths and overcome your weaknesses.
- Find and list out the negative traits that hinder your progress and discard the same gradually.
- Always love changes and challenges.
- Be free from *'fear of failure'* or *'fear of criticism'*.
- Don't envelope in desperation and develop insecurities.

- Never strive for perfection but only excellence.
- Never compare yourself with others. You are what you are and God created you with a specific mission in this world.
- Avoid negative environment.
- Never brood over past failures. Always think of what next whenever you face failures.
- Avoid rumormongers, naggers, backstabbers, sluffers, snipers and whiners,
- Always be positive and confident.
- Forgive and forget.
- Stay away from procrastination.
- Finally, find out your talents and tap them. Develop your skills and abilities and leverage your inborn talents with cultivated skills and abilities for achieving all-round success.

Roadmap to Your Self-Improvement Plan

The biggest room in the world is the room for improvement. - Author Unknown

Daily get up early at a fixed time and start your day. It is possible through self-discipline. Plan what you intend to do for the rest of the day. It makes things less complex as you have already planned. Many successful entrepreneurs and personalities get up early at a fixed time. Go for a brisk walk or hit gym or do meditation as it fills you with energy and enthusiasm. It is the key to your self improvement.

Go ahead the day with the to-do list by setting priorities. Sometimes there will be external disturbances which sidetrack your plans. Don't get disheartened. Address the disturbances and get back to your track with renewed energy and enthusiasm.

Manage your time judiciously by addressing the tasks based on priority of importance. Never hold grudges against others as it kills your time in thinking about them as well as ruining your healthy mind. Cultivate the attitude of *'forgive and forget'* which is possible only when you shed the past negative events and experiences about others. Research reveals that people waste 30 percent of their precious time by thinking about their bitter past which cannot be altered. Charles F. Kettering rightly quotes, "You can't have a better tomorrow if you are thinking about yesterday all the time." Therefore, the wisdom lies in looking and living at the present and proceeding further without any regrets.

Takeaways

Become addicted to constant and never ending self improvement. - Anthony J. D'Angelo

You need to have right strategy, practical action and consistency in approach in achieving success. While executing the tasks for a long time and if you miss in reaching your goals then it is time to take stock of the situation and strategy and follow a different course of action. Possess right tools and techniques in achieving your goals and objectives.

You cannot have success in overnight. Even if success comes in overnight, it would fade away within no time. Always be prepared. You don't know when you will get opportunity. You will regret if you don't rise to the occasion when opportunity knocks at your door. Therefore, invest every moment through continuous self-improvement for achieving success.

SELF-AWARENESS

The more you know, the less you need to show. - Anonymous

There are several ingredients essential for achieving success. Of which, self-awareness is one, which is key to success. People are more comfortable in knowing about others than about themselves. A few people have the habit of complaining, condemning and criticizing others' behavior and nature. They cannot digest when others think and behave with them as superiors. In fact, nobody is perfect in this world. We all have our strengths and weaknesses and being aware of the same will help us to become successful persons.

What is Self-Awareness?

He who knows others is wise. He who knows himself is enlightened. - Lao Tzu

Self-awareness is all about knowing oneself thoroughly such as attitudes, aptitude, needs, desires, goals, habits, emotions, strengths and weaknesses etc., In brief, it means knowing your personality. Self-awareness is nothing but being conscious about yourself and how you act and react in certain situations.

We all have low level of awareness but think that we know about ourselves better. It is, in fact, wrong. When you know yourself properly, you judge yourself properly and you take your judgments seriously. It requires lot of self-knowledge to be aware of yourself.

Merits of Self-Awareness

Don't bother just to be better than your contemporaries or predecessors. Try to be better than yourself. - William Faulkner

- People with self-awareness stands at better chances of winning the game because they know about themselves. If any mistake is made, they immediately take remedial action as they know about themselves.
- Self-Awareness improves your judgment and decision making skills. It helps in developing your personality as you overcome your weaknesses.
- It bridges the gap between skills you have and you don't have and exploits your existing skills up to the hilt.
- It helps in choosing the right career and ensures fast career growth.
- When you know more about yourself, most of the problems in your life are resolved automatically.
- You can become a successful mentor, facilitator, teacher, leader and role model with better self-awareness.

How to Know About Yourself

It's surprising how many persons go through life without ever recognizing that their feelings toward other people are largely determined by their feelings toward themselves, and if you're not comfortable within yourself, you can't be comfortable with others. - Sydney J. Harris

- Take time to think things through. Spend some time to analyze yourself. Self-introspection is essential to be aware about yourself.

- Go for MBTI (Meyers and Briggs Type Instrument) test as it helps you find out what type of personality you are.
- There are several psychometric instruments to know your personality. When such instruments are executed by professional trainers then it becomes easier to know more about yourself.
- Take feedback from your colleagues, friends and relatives. Take their feedback separately so that the common qualities running across the thread can be taken as the correct characteristics.
- Go for meditation as it reveals about your mind. Or go to a serene place and think about yourself to take stock of your qualities.
- Take a notebook and write down your thoughts, ideas and insights. Record the same for analysis and evaluation.
- Take intrapersonal feedback regularly. For this, it is essential to engage in regular inner dialogue.
- Constantly monitor your actions and its fall out.
- Take the help of professional counselors, clinical psychologists and executive coaches who can provide you correct feedback. Find out the inventory of your interests and personality that help in developing your self-awareness.

Ken's Honest Feedback about Susan

Everything that irritates us about others can lead us to an understanding of ourselves. — Carl Gustav Jung

People have tendency to judge others. But they don't accept when others judge them. Rather they would be shocked with others' feedback about themselves. Let us look at an example where two colleagues by names, Susan and Ken who worked in an office. They had good relations and gelled with each other well. One day, Susan asked Ken to give feedback as she wanted to know about herself from the perspective of Ken. Ken was straightforward by nature and he analyzed Susan from several dimensions both personally and professionally and prepared a report containing her strengths and weaknesses. It took around a week for Ken to generate the personality report of Susan. He went to the extent of guessing the MBTI personality type of Susan based on her behavior, nature and intellectual temperament.

When Susan saw the report she could not digest and she did not agree with Ken on several areas. Ken clearly said that he was not perfect in assessment but offered feedback the way he provided to several students when he worked as a faculty member in a Business School. Since then, Susan distanced from Ken as she never expected her nature to be like that. It led to severance of their amicable relations and finally costing their friendship. The lesson to be learnt in this context is that people don't accept about themselves when others offer their feedback because they think about themselves in a different manner. In fact, there is always gap between an individual's imagination about himself/herself with that of others.

Takeaways

The final mystery is oneself. - Oscar Wilde

Self-awareness is all about being aware of your intentions, actions, emotions, feelings, attitude and aptitude so that you can channel them successfully for achieving all round success.

When you know yourself well you grow as a true individual. You develop self-acceptance which in turn helps others to accept you as an individual. You become self motivated and it leads to achieving success. Self-awareness enables you to grow in your chosen area of interest. To sum up, success comes to those who have better self-awareness about themselves as it helps in improving themselves by overcoming their weaknesses and reinforcing their strengths.

SELF-ESTEEM

I am very special, unique, and valuable person. I deserve to feel good about myself.

Boosting self-esteem is very easy when you know what is all about self-esteem. Having self-esteem promotes the prospects of your success personally, professionally and socially. It is an essential component of success in every stage of life such as childhood, adolescence, and youth and in old age. It is rightly said by Beth Graney, guidance at Bull Run Middle School in Gainesvile, Virginia that, "Adults achieve self-esteem from their achievements, the adolescents achieve from their group and kids achieve from their peer relationships." Before we look at boosting self-esteem let us find out what is all about self-esteem.

What is Self-Esteem?

According to Goleman author of the book titled 'Emotional Intelligence', "Self-esteem or self-efficacy has to do with a realistic assessment of your strengths and weaknesses".

When you feel bad about yourself from time to time you have low self-esteem. In contrast, when you feel good about yourself constantly you have high self-esteem. Self-esteem means having pride in oneself and self-respect. It is a state of thinking where one feels good about oneself. Self-esteem is all about feeling good of oneself every time whether in success or failure.

Self-esteem should not be confused with self-confidence which is related to self-beliefs and sense of being able to do something successfully. Self-esteem should not also be confused with self-efficacy which is related to certain abilities, capabilities and competencies to move towards future performance. The concept is believed to have been coined by John Milton. Self-esteem is one of the important ingredients for success. It is our ability to value ourselves. It is the overall opinion we have about ourselves. When you think that you are competent then you have appropriate self-esteem *i.e.*, high self-esteem and when you think that you are not competent then you have inappropriate self-esteem *i.e.*, low self-esteem.

Self-esteem comes from a sense of our own worth. It is based on true awareness of our strengths and weaknesses, combined with acceptance that human beings are, by nature, a mixture of such qualities. We are living in a society that is continually being impacted by the symptoms and side effects of low self-esteem.

Abraham Maslow's Hierarchy of Needs

Abraham Maslow, an American psychologist, developed hierarchy of needs where in after fulfilling one level of needs, human beings will be motivated to reach the next higher order of needs. For instance, human beings look basically for meeting physiological needs like food, cloth, shelter, sex etc. While working, employees look for rest periods, work breaks, lunch breaks etc., The second higher level of needs is the safety and security needs where human beings like to be free from fear of physical, psychological and financial needs. At workplace, the employees look for job security, pension benefits, insurance etc., to secure themselves. The third higher level of needs is the social needs where they crave for love and affection and affiliation with their communities and groups. While working in organizations, they like to work in groups by forming teams which is the right example for social needs. After fulfilling these needs they crave for esteem needs such as they expect respect and recognition from others. Hike in their pay and perks, promotions and having company car can promote their self-esteem needs. The top highest hierarchy of needs is the self-actualization needs where they want to have freedom to be creative and innovative and want to pursue their passionate areas of interest. When the employees are encouraged to take up higher roles and responsibilities they enjoy accepting the challenges as they derive immense pleasure out of it.

From the above hierarchy of needs, we find the self-esteem has place for itself which is indication of its importance in human motivation and needs.

Causes

Self pity is our worst enemy and if we yield to it, we can never do anything wise in the world. - Helen Keller

Nobody is born with low self-esteem. Parents, educational institutions and society are responsible for creating low self-esteem among people. When our thoughts constantly rotate and revolve around the deficiencies, shortcomings, weaknesses and insecurities, we tend to develop low self-esteem. Besides, frequent failures and criticism by others may lead to self-doubt resulting into depression and anxiety. Inferiority complex among the people may give rise to low self-esteem. When people are not good looking they tend to think low of themselves resulting into low self-esteem. Parents are also responsible to some extent for low self-esteem among their children when they have unrealistic aspirations and expectations from their children.

Effects

Low self-esteem prevents you from enjoying life, doing the thing you want to do, and working towards your personal and professional goals. It adversely affects your relations with others. One can observe anxiety, depression, insomnia, substance abuse and other self-destructive behaviors. It also gives rise to self-doubt and self-criticism. When you have low self-esteem you give in yourself to negative self-talk, like *"I am not smart"*.

Strategies to Boost Your Self-Esteem

Outstanding leaders go out of their way to boost the self-esteem of their personnel. If people believe in themselves, it's amazing what they can accomplish. - Sam Walton

- Love yourself first. Only when you start loving yourself then you can expect others to love you.
- Develop a healthy and positive mindset for boosting self-esteem.
- Set smart, measurable, achievable, realistic and timed (SMART) goals. Right goals take you towards right direction resulting into one success after another success culminating into higher self-esteem.
- Pursue your passionate areas of interest. Carefully listen to your head and heart and synchronize the same to build self-esteem.

- Take care of your physical, mental and emotional health. Hit gym regularly or go for jogging or swimming or walking to distress yourself. Read good books which provide you enough mental diet. And balance yourself emotionally.
- Concentrate on your strengths rather than weaknesses. Prepare a list of your weaknesses and work on to improve slowly and steadily.
- Create positive circle of friends who respect you and your areas of interest so that you can boost your self-esteem.
- Always explore the ways and means to tap your inner talents and also develop skills as the combination these two will help you to look at the world with positive attitude.
- Always start from where you are strong as it builds your self-confidence.
- Attend workshops or seminars as it widens your intellectual horizons.
- List out and recall your past achievements. Also, list out positive affirmations and read the same daily when you get up from bed in the morning and go to bed in the night. Once it is done for a period of a month, then you find amazing results.
- Substitute your negative thoughts with positive ones. Keep busy with your commitments and goals. It helps in minimizing negative thoughts and maximizing positive thoughts. It will also help you stay focused.
- Never compare yourself with others as you are unique and different. Always focus on your unique innate traits and characteristics and also the things you like.
- Always compete with yourself and raise your bar gradually.
- Take someone you like the most as a role model so that you can draw motivation and inspiration.
- Always involve yourself in positive self-talk. Everyone has an inner dialogue. Always think internally that you are born to do great things and you are sure to achieve the same. Constant inner dialogue reinforces positive self-talk resulting into feeling good about yourself.
- Learn from failures and move forward. Never underestimate nor overestimate yourself.
- Don't hold your anger inside. Once anger is held then it would explode like volcano. Find out what angers you and let go your angry emotions by expressing as it relieves your inner burden. Express yourself to close friends what causes you anger.
- Care less about others and especially for their unhealthy criticism. Les Brown rightly said, "Someone's opinion of you does not have to become your reality."
- Be kind and helpful to others. When you do so, people respect your positive gesture which in turn raises your self-esteem.
- Develop the attitude of forgetting any negative events or experiences in life and forgiving others.
- Children should focus on academic excellence and extra-curricular activities and achievements as these promote high self-esteem.
- Strive for excellence not perfection.
- Cultivate the hobby of gifting.
- Practice smiling as it improves your face value.
- Build your inner strengths which helps in enhancing your physical, mental, emotional and spiritual strength.

- Do what you love to do rather than loving what you do. There is a thin line separating these two. When you do what you love to do you enjoy every moment resulting into higher self-esteem.
- Be assertive - excessive high self-esteem leads to aggressiveness and low self-esteem results in submissiveness. Therefore, it is essential to maintain the average of both behaviors which is possible by assertiveness.
- Always be grateful to God for what has been given to you. Develop the attitude of gratitude.

Takeaways

Sooner or later, those who win are those who think they can. - Richard Bach

Low self-esteem is not a problem by birth. It is injected by various ways and means. In some cases, it is due to parental influence. The faulty social and educational environment also aggravates this problem. The fact is that self-esteem can be learned, taught, developed and spread. Let us teach kids to feel good about themselves in their childhood itself so that they grow and live with high self-esteem in later part of their lives. To sum up, respect yourself, reward yourself, honor yourself, love yourself and feel good about yourself for boosting your self-esteem.

SELF-CONFIDENCE

If you think that you can do it then it is confidence, if you think that you can alone do it then it is overconfidence. There is a thin line separating self-confidence from over-confidence.

Confidence is the key to overcome trials and tribulations in life. It is one of the most important aspects which help in moving forward in life. Confidence is the ability to have full faith in oneself to face the fight and to take it forward to its logical end. Confidence comes when you make the things happen not when you let the things happen. It helps in touching you upper limits. It brings inner satisfaction, happiness and joy.

Confidence is an inner voice which tells us what we can do. Confidence does not mean overrating or overestimating than that of others. It is neither feeling superior nor great but feeling comfortable with convictions. Confidence is the ability to assess and judge yourself properly. It is also the ability not to underestimate your rivals or competitors. Confidence is essential everywhere. For instance, a leader needs confidence to lead team, a student needs confidence to score higher marks and a teacher needs confidence to speak in front of students.

What is Self-Confidence?

Be who you are and say what you feel, because those who mind don't matter and those who matter don't mind. - Dr. Seuss

Self-confidence comes from competence, competence comes from experience and experience comes from hard work, expertise, practice, knowledge, skills and abilities. It is mental attitude where in individuals have to believe in themselves, respect themselves, rely on their abilities, capabilities, competencies, and intuition.

Confidence and optimism are two sides of the same coin. For achieving success in any sphere, it is necessary to equip with these two traits. Self-confident people take risks and accept roles and responsibilities voluntarily. They take on the battle to its logical end without any fear or self-doubt. They would face the fight and would fight to the finish.

When we look at all successful people, it transpires that they all have great self-confidence. We tend to think that their success led them to have self-confidence. We can say that prior to success it was their self-confidence that led to success and not the other way round.

There are number of people who started from nowhere and reached to number one status due to their confidence. There are people who rose like phoenix despite failures because of their self-confidence.

John's Overconfidence

If you don't make mistakes then you are a perfect human and if you make mistakes then you are a human. - Farouk

John was highly educated and was good at his job. Due to recession the entire department was closed. Finally the axe fell on John also to leave the organization. Before being axed, the employer provided outplacement to John to join in one of their affiliates where his services could be utilized. John was overconfident and said the employer that he had couple of offers and would shortlist the same and get back to them. On hearing this, the employer provided the opportunity to one of his colleagues.

After closure of establishment John had to struggle for a suitable employment for a month as the job market was weak due to recession. John had ability and capability to get better employment and finally settled down for an employment as per his passion. Only regret he had was to remain unemployed for a month and he lost a salary for that period. Had John accepted the previous employer's offer he would have worked there and would have tried for better opportunities by working in that organization. John's over-confidence led to losing salary for a period of one month and undergoing mental trauma without job. Let us accept the fact that over-confidence is the worst enemy.

Signs of Self-Confident People

A self-confident person grabs the opportunities whereas an over-confident person rejects the available opportunities. Let us look at the signs and signals of self-confident people.

1. Never doubt their competencies, capabilities, abilities and skills.
2. Have total command and control over themselves.
3. Are risk takers and love to live on edge.
4. Humility is their hallmark.
5. Have neither superiority nor inferiority complex. They possess the right complex desired for success.
6. Are open to new areas of interests, challenges and changes in life.
7. Are ready to test new waters by assuming challenging roles and responsibilities.
8. Have clarity of mind and approach towards problem solving.
9. Are ready to take constructive criticism in their stride and strive for continuous feedback.
10. Have tenacity and resilience to overcome from failures.
11. Have an attitude to strive for excellence, not perfection.

Tips for Building Self-Confidence

Will power is essential to build confidence as it enables a person to do anything and everything that leads to success.

- Self-belief is the first and foremost things towards building self-confidence.
- Take up the tasks which are little more difficult and start executing them. Over a period of time, you will develop self-confidence.
- Learning is the key to self-confidence. If you learn swimming, then you develop self-confidence gradually to get into water next time. Similarly, learn new skills and abilities so that you will develop competencies and capabilities which lead to developing self-confidence.
- Always radiate positive energy and enthusiasm.
- Always have positive self-affirmations everyday such as *'I am great', 'I will succeed', 'I was born to achieve big in this world'* and so on.
- List out your achievements in life and keep adding fresh ones along with the existing one. It is like updating your resume while applying for employment. It will enhance confidence levels as it generates positive vibes.
- Substitute your negative thoughts with positive ones. Always think that you are winner and you would achieve everything in life. When your mind is filled with positive ideas, thoughts and information then you develop confidence and it leads to success.
- Everyone is blessed with unique talents and traits. Find out where you are strong at, tap and explore the same for achieving success.
- Take timely food. Hit gym or do meditation regularly. Positive mind in a healthy body will enhance confidence levels.
- Always involve in positive self-talk. But don't make it excess as it leads to blowing your own trumpet. Therefore, keep your positive self-talk within the healthy limits.
- Don't unduly concern what others think about you. You are what you are and you are unique and incomparable with others. Therefore, care less about others. Don't focus on unhealthy criticism.
- Don't worry too much about your past failures. Failures are common in life. It indicates that you have attempted to achieve something in life. Learn lessons from failures and just move on towards success.
- Always be faithful to your conscience and possess strong character. There is an age-old proverb and it goes, "Confession is good for the soul". If you did wrong it is better to own up and confess as it relieves your burden to your conscience. Conscience reflects the ethical values while character demonstrates both the emotional and ethical values. These two are the driving forces towards building better self-confidence.

Takeaways

You are what you think about all day long. - Dr. Robert Schuller

Self-confidence is not a born quality. It is a cultivated trait by external environment. It is inculcated by parents and educational institutions during upbringing. Besides, social environment always plays a vital role in building this trait. To sum up, let us admit the fact that everyone is born with the ability to instinctively achieve something in life and it is the self-confidence that finally helps in achieving success.

SELF-DISCIPLINE

If you do not conquer self, you will be conquered by self. - Napoleon Hill

What is Self-Discipline?

Self-discipline means training oneself to stick to code of conduct or behavior although the person is willing to do something else at heart but he does as he is expected to do it. Self-discipline is a trait, habit and a skill. It requires consistent efforts to remain self-disciplined. In fact, consistency is the key to self-discipline. Self-discipline needs struggles and sacrifices. Success springs from such strenuous efforts and energies.

Self-discipline is a voluntary and conscious effort to discipline oneself without any external influence. For instance, being punctual to work rather being reminded by others to be on time, being focused in work voluntarily rather being prompted by superiors, getting up early in the morning regularly without anybody's coercion and getting the tasks executed without procrastination can be considered self-discipline.

Self-discipline is sticking to tight schedules, rules and regulations without anybody's influence and coercion. In a nut shell, being duty-conscious, being punctual, being conscious of others, being organized and being initiative are the bedrock for self-discipline. It must go deep within the subconscious mind. It is like minding one's own work without being reminded by others.

Self-discipline is combination of self-control, self-command, self-regulation and self-feedback. Hitting gym regularly, taking timely food and leading a systematic life become the bedrock of self-discipline.

If you want to decrease your weight, you need to hit the gym. You need to have will power to pursue hitting gym relentlessly for shedding the excess flab. If you are a diabetic and the doctor instructs you to avoid taking sugar then you need to display self-discipline to stick to the instructions.

Will Power and Self-Discipline

Will power and self-discipline are two sides of the same coin. While will power helps in overcoming laziness and procrastination, self-discipline helps in developing stamina, endurance, resilience and tenacity, perseverance and motivation. When you are equipped with these two traits you will be confident of taking the things forward. Both are investments for future success.

Merits of Self-Discipline

Self-discipline is an act of cultivation. It requires you to connect today's actions to tomorrow's results. There's a season for sowing a season for reaping. Self-discipline helps you know which is which. - Gary Ryan Blair

Self-discipline empowers your personality. It equips you with several tools and techniques that help in achieving success. It makes you stand out. It makes you rise from the rest. It will project you as a leader who stands different from others. There are many merits associated with self-discipline. Let us look at few of them.

1. It helps in organizing people better as it makes them to get up from sleep at regular times and do things in systematic and focused manner.

2. It enhances the personality of the individuals thus projecting in a positive manner.
3. It is stepping stone towards success.
4. It helps in achieving your goals much faster and smarter.

Inculcating Self-Discipline

In reading the lives of great men, I found that the first victory they won was over themselves... self-discipline with all of them came first. - Harry S. Truman

- Maintain good friends who fuel you with positive thoughts and ideas. Positive company of friends keeps you healthy thus making you self-disciplined.
- Cultivate the habit of maintaining diary. Jot down the ideas that surface from your mind. Don't rely on your memory. It is rightly said that a short pencil is better than a long memory. Jotting down the key ideas enhances perseverance as well.
- Take up one task at a time and do it. Don't mix up several tasks as you end up no where. It will stay you focused and make you task oriented.
- Break big tasks into small ones. When you find a big task you may feel like giving up assuming as the difficult one. But when you break it down then work slowly and steadily by addressing small pieces then you will be able to achieve your goal easily however big it might be. When you follow this strategy you will find amazing results. Henry Ford rightly said, "Nothing is particularly hard if you divide it into small jobs".
- Face the problems rather than avoiding them. Face the fight and take the battle of life to its logical end. It is the secret of self-discipline.
- It is always better to do than to do well in life. Never focus on perfection but on excellence.
- Always put work before pleasure. Once the work is over then you can concentrate on pleasure. Else, you would not enjoy the pleasure as your mind is concerned about work.
- Always push yourself harder beyond your limits so that the best within you will come out.
- Set small goals and try to achieve. Once you achieve small goals, then you develop a flow that will encourage you to become self-disciplined.
- Set your own standards and never compare with others. Realize the fact that everyone is unique.
- Active participation in sports and games will develop self-discipline.
- Learn to associate with positive activities and experiences as these encourage people to be self-disciplined.

Takeaways

It is not fair to ask of others what you are not willing to do yourself. - Eleanor Roosevelt

The poor self-discipline makes you weak and unsuccessful and over discipline makes you sacrifice your personal happiness and joy. Therefore, learn to strike the right balance between the both for reaching greater heights in your life.

You can do anything and everything through self-discipline. People with self-discipline rarely give up. They place work before pleasure. After completion of the work they enjoy the pleasure without any guilt feeling.

Self-discipline is a skill not a talent. Therefore, it is easy to cultivate the skill of self-discipline. It requires will power, stamina and endurance to acquire this skill. The educational institutions can play a crucial role in shaping the students through self-discipline. Similarly, the role of parents is also appreciated to inculcate the skill among their children.

Self-discipline determines the destiny of the individuals. It holds the key to success. Successful people cultivate this quality from their childhood itself. To sum up, life without self-discipline is like a ship sailing without navigation.

SELF-DETERMINATION

Strength does not come from physical capacity. It comes from an indomitable will. - Mahatma Gandhi.

What is Self-Determination?

Self-determination is a cluster of several skills, abilities, knowledge, beliefs, traits and talents that enable people to engage themselves with tons of self-confidence. It comes from your inner strength and courage. It helps to take on the challenges and changes in life with head on. It strengthens your inner belief to take the battle to its logical end. Self-determination is something hidden which can be demonstrated through actions not by external appearance.

Importance

The difference between a successful person and others is not a lack of strength, not a lack of knowledge, but rather a lack of will. - Vincent T. Lombardi

Self-determination is necessary to succeed in life. Self-determination helps in equipping you with necessary strength and courage to meet the day-to-day challenges in your life. Hannibal rightly said, "We will either find a way or make one."

Self-determination is required to break your conditioned thinking. People, by continuous reading and experience, tend to develop a particular mindset which is hard to break. As the world is changing rapidly with changing technology, people have to develop adaptability to survive in the cut throat competitive world. Self-determination plays a crucial role in breaking the traditional barriers and boundaries.

How to Build?

Every man is the architect of his own fortune. - Sallust

- Take an ideal and successful person as a role model and draw inspiration.
- Don't let past failures haunt you. Learn lessons from failures and try again with optimism and confidence.
- Always look for positive elements in every adversity, defeat or sorrow.
- Be clear about your goals and vision. Find out what you want clearly and create a blueprint to achieve.
- Be sympathetic and empathetic with others.
- Concentrate only on your efforts and energies, not on results.
- Monitor your progress and take continuous feedback.

- Take care of your mental and physical health.
- Never entertain cynicism and pessimism to creep in your mind.
- Always look for solutions and don't brood too much on problems.
- And finally trust in God.

Takeaways

I don't know what the future may hold, but I know who holds the future. - Ralph Abernathy

Self-determination helps you build your hidden potential and you can unleash the same for achieving all-round success as and when required. It is a magical key to success. It turns your adversities into opportunities. To put it in the words of Edward Gibbon, "The winds and waves are always on the side of the ablest navigators." To sum up, self-determination helps you in becoming an influential personality thus bringing difference in the lives of others.

SELF-MOTIVATION

Don't' let the low times keep you down. Learn from them and reach for the high times. - David Wiemers.

What is Self-Motivation?

Self motivation is the ability to motivate yourself without the influence of others. It is the ability to move forward with your convictions and beliefs despite facing several stumbling blocks on your way. It is also the ability to move forward with energy and enthusiasm without any letup. It radiates firm faith in yourself. It is the courage to follow your convictions. It is all about not letting other's opinions drown out your inner beliefs. It is one of the important aspects for achieving success.

People are motivated through different ways and means such as reading books, money, love, comfort, career, success etc., Therefore, it is essential to find out how you are motivated so that the process of self-motivation becomes easier.

Merits of Self-Motivation

- It keeps your energy levels always higher. It develops optimism and confidence which are keys to your success.
- Self-motivation makes you think *'what next'* whenever faced with failures. It reminds you that failure is only a comma not a full stop.
- It reduces absenteeism and labor turnover in organizations thus increasing performance and productivity.
- It creates conducive work environment.
- It saves time, money and energy.
- It brings all round progress and prosperity for individuals and institutions.

Secrets of Self-Motivation

People become really quite remarkable when they start thinking that they can do things. When they believe in themselves they have the first secret of success. - Norman Vincent Peale

Dream big: You need to think big always which is possible only when you dream big. Dreams will drive you to go to any extent. Your efforts and energies towards your goals totally depend on your level of dreams. Sigmund Freud rightly quoted, "Man dreams only that which he has the ability to achieve."

Set a roadmap: Mere having dreams will not pay off unless you have blueprint towards achieving the same. The blueprint should be so planned that it should be realistic and practical to achieve. Find out what are your inborn talents and combine the same with the skills and abilities that you acquired through training, practice and experience.

Be a firm optimist: When you develop positive attitude round the clock you tend to have positive results. This positive thought process leads to positive actions by blocking negative aspects. It drives you towards achieving your goals by looking at the brighter side of life.

You are unique: Begin everyday with new expectations and aspirations. Stay away from negative thoughts and negative people. Accept the fact that you are unique and cannot be compared with others. Have a firm faith that you were born to achieve big in this world.

Involve in internal dialogue: This is a powerful tool where your talk to yourself and reinforce yourself. Internal dialogue helps in strengthening your subconscious mind by feeding with right inputs.

Pursue your passions: Passion is a burning desire coming from the core of your heart. It is like your heart prevailing over your mind. It is all about doing what you love to do. Find out what interests you and work on it. It propels you in moving forward when several odds stacked against you.

Set your goals: Sheila Murray Bethel quotes, "One of the most courageous things you can do is identify yourself, know who you are, what you believe in and where you want to go." When you set your goals based on your desires, you develop positive attitude towards life and your mind is engaged in a right way. You will have a clearer vision about what you want to do for planning your mission. Break the goals into short term and long term and link both in such a way that they should be correlated and interconnected without any contradiction. As you achieve your goals you get self-motivated. Even if there is failure in accomplishing your short term goals due to external disturbances, the long term goals will hold you firmly with faith thus motivating you forever.

Break your goals: When you feel that your goal is too big, make it into small and keep achieving it one by one. Once you achieve a small goal you get motivated over your achievement and will be driven to work further and forward. When you complete all sub-goals confidently then you will be excited to know that you have achieved your big goal successfully.

Consistency is the key: Chuck Norris says, "If you want to accomplish anything in life, you can't just sit back and hope it will happen. You've got to make it happen." Put your efforts and energies in a systematic and focused manner without looking for results frequently. Your objective is to put in efforts regularly. Consistency with a firm commitment is the key to self-motivation and success.

Manage your time: Learn to manage your time effectively and efficiently by allocating specific time for each activity. Invest your time on daily basis for each activity without encroaching into other activities. Avoid procrastination. Delaying the activities will result into lethargy and piling up the activities resulting into stress.

High energy levels: Always maintain high energy levels. Take good and nutritious food. Avoid junk food. Take food at regular intervals everyday. Hit gym or go for fast walking to lift your energy levels. High energy levels will keep you highly motivated.

Focus on solutions, not problems: Never focus too much on problems. Generally, people brood over the problems and waste their precious time. Look for solutions towards the problems. It is rightly said that below average people talk about individuals, average people talk about events, issues and problems and above average people always talk about ideas and solutions.

Spend time with loved ones: When you spend your time weekends with your family and friends you rejuvenate your energies. You create and strengthen your emotional bonding. When you spend your time one day in a week with your spouse, you develop better understanding by sharing your feelings and emotions. Similarly, when you spend a day in a week with your children you share your love with them thereby building bridges. Besides, you can educate as well as develop them as individuals with strong character with values. You can also play with kids as they are innocent and lovely. It removes your stress and fills you with self-motivation.

Never give up: Walter Sparrow, Now and Then, says, "Things will happen in your life that you can't stop, but that's no reason to shut out the world. There's a purpose for the good and for the bad." Hold on to your cherished goals and objectives. There will be several challenges while executing your tasks throwing you out of the gear. Be firm and strong and ensure that the things are put on the right and fast track. It is rightly said, winners don't quit and quitters never win.

Takeaways

Go confidently in the direction of your dreams. Live the life you have imagined. - Henry David Thoreau

Self-motivation helps you in achieving anything you desire. Channel your burning desire to achieve whatever you want. When you are enthusiastic and excited about what you are doing and when you are motivated, committed and dedicated you are sure to achieve success. Make a resolution to motivate one individual everyday. Make a difference in the lives of people. To conclude, self-motivation gears you to accomplish your desires for achieving all-round success. It is a bridge between your dreams and realities.

SELF-CONTROL

An excessively ambitious man and an overly aggressive woman never live in peace and prosperity. - Prof. M.S.Rao

What is Self-Control?

Self-control is all about altering one's own attitudes, behaviors, personality in tune with expectations and standards of the society in order to achieve one's goals and objectives. Failing so, it results into rejection by society. It requires great mental energies and efforts to possess self-control.

Self-control is like self-mastery. It is absence of anger, intolerance and impulsiveness. You may compare your body with a chariot, your mind with reigns and your intellect with driver. Self-control means controlling your mind and body. You can achieve anything through self-control. You need to control all your five senses such as sight sound, smell, taste and touch to have total control on yourself.

Merits of Self-Control

Self control gives you peace of mind, ensures better relations with others thereby giving you competitive edge over others. Better self-control leads to higher self-esteem, better interpersonal skills and emotional intelligence. It will earn you respect and goodwill in the society. It makes you simple and humble. Overall, self-control enhances the personality of individuals thus taking them through the righteous path. People reached from nowhere to number one position though sheer self-control.

Demerits Due to Dearth of Self-Control

It is difficult to raise high in life. And it is very easy to fall free in life. Lack of self-control has several demerits. People resort to drugs, smoking, alcohol, crimes and violence, impulsive behavior and unwanted pregnancy due to lack of self-control. Individuals lose self-respect and dignity in the society. They may be subjected to humiliation and insults from others. People may get into wrong path. Those who do not have self-control don't enjoy reputation. A few celebrities involve into controversies. Although it may be good to get instant publicity to promote themselves, it demonstrates their lack of self-control and it will harm them in the long run. History reveals several great leaders getting into abyss due to lack of self-control.

Tips for Better Self-Control

- We are human beings with emotions. When emotions cloud reasoning, we will be driven over the edge. Don't be impulsive. Hold back yourself. Lack of self-control results into a moment of madness and lifetime regret. Don't be unduly emotional. Learn to utilize your emotions effectively.
- Do meditation regularly to have better control over your mind.
- Feed your subconscious mind with positive thoughts.
- Hypnotize your mind that you have adequate self-control.
- Control your behavior as per the expected standards and benchmarks.
- Take intrapersonal and interpersonal feedback regularly for building self-control.

Susan's Anger and Ron's Self-Control

Friends are made by many acts...and lost by only one. — Harvey Mackay

In an office two colleagues by name Susan and Ron worked amicably. Susan was senior in the office while Ron was junior although the latter was elder to the former in age. Besides, Ron was more experienced when clubbed with his past experience in other areas when compared with Susan. Both Ron and Susan were good by nature, but Susan was a stubborn and dominant woman. She always dictated others as she was the senior most in the department. However, both maintained good friendship.

Once there was a task assigned by Susan where in Ron was asked to collect the documents of other departments and were to be handed over to HR department. Under the instructions of Susan, Ron collected and handed over to Tony in the HR department. But what Susan meant was to hand over the same to a specific person John in HR department. In fact, Susan and Tony did not gel with each other.

On hearing that the documents were handed over to Tony, Susan burst into anger and shouted at Ron. Ron tried to remind Susan that the documents were handed over as instructed. Susan lost her self-control and took Ron to task about the issue. Ron repeatedly tried to persuade Susan that it was not an issue to blow up in proportions. He went on further by telling her that Susan would have specifically communicated to hand over the same to John. Ron was a cool and mature man and somehow managed to control the temper of Susan about the improper communication. From thereafter, both Ron and Susan had strained relations and departed forever. From this example it becomes very clear about the importance of self-control.

Takeaways

Acquire knowledge as knowledge is power. It will help in strengthening your self-control. Those who are highly focused and task oriented have better self-control than others. Leaders demonstrate their self-control during success and defeat. Self-control is a skill. It is not a trait or talent that one is born with. It is possible by changing your behavior through practice. Everything is in your mind. Therefore, control your mind so that you can control everything within and around you for achieving all-round success.

PUNCTUALITY

I could never think well of a man's intellectual or moral character, if he was habitually unfaithful to his appointments. - Nathaniel Emmons

How do you feel when your flight is delayed throwing your entire plans out of gear? How do you feel when a patient dies due to the unpunctuality of a doctor? How do you feel when you miss a job opportunity due to the delay of your car driver? How do you feel when you find people who are late and don't have the elementary courtesy of expressing regret for their delay? Imagine and think. You get annoyed over the people for not being punctual resulting into several implications and complications.

What is Punctuality?

Punctuality is the politeness of kings. - Louis XVIII

Punctuality is a habit where an individual does things on time. It is one of the secrets for success and one of the hallmarks of leaders. Punctuality means being systematic maintaining everything in orderly manner and completing the task and being available on time. Punctuality is etiquette. Punctuality is all about doing things timely and being aware of the importance of time. It helps in managing ones own time thereby respecting others' as well.

Punctuality is also doing things timely and being aware of the importance of time. It helps in managing ones own time thereby respecting others as well. Being punctual is a sign of discipline. Defence personnel are trained to be disciplined and are punctual. They stick to punctuality whether it is rain or shine. Succinctly, it is an attitude to be on time as per schedules.

Advantages of Punctuality

I have always been a quarter of an hour before my time, and it has made a man of me. - Lord Horatio Nelson

Punctuality helps in better time management, time discipline and it projects and presents your personality positively to others. It indicates how much concern and respect you have towards others to whom you have given your appointment. It is like valuing others and their time and sends right signals for others. You don't have to cut a sorry figure for being late when you are punctual.

If you know how to manage your time properly then you will learn how to be punctual. When people maintain punctuality, work can be executed smoothly and successfully. If people don't stick to deadlines, they tend to procrastinate culminating into delays and stress. If you are punctual you can avoid stress and anxiety and gain respect among others. If people waste one minute of their time they are wasting one minute of their life. In a nut shell, punctuality saves your precious time as well as others. You command respect among all. You will have peace of mind as things roll out as per the schedule. Finally, you can be in the good books of all.

Causes

The trouble with being punctual is that nobody's there to appreciate it. - Jones, Franklin P.

Excessive work may result into postponement thereby delaying other activities. Lack of seriousness on the part of individuals and taking things lightly may result into procrastination. When people don't maintain diary they don't remember the program schedule. In few cases, people forget their commitments and appointments as they are preoccupied with other activities. Improper planning of work may lead to accumulation of the tasks resulting into further delays. Finally, when people are not smart at time management skills, it may lead to unpunctuality.

Effects

If I have made an appointment with you, I owe you punctuality, I have no right to throw away your time, if I do my own. - Cecil Richard

The repercussions of unpunctuality are many such as building up tension resulting into stress and fatigue. It brings disrespect to the individuals and they lose their name, fame and dignity. It is very difficult for these people to climb the ladder of success at the workplace. If you delay by 15 minutes and the people waiting for you, for instance, are 10 then you wasted 150 minutes of their precious time. Is it proper to make others' time unproductive?

Tips to be Punctual

We are not saints, but we have kept our appointment. How many people can boast as much? - Beckett Samuel

- Develop a positive mindset to be punctual.
- Initially, it requires lot of practice to be punctual.
- Set your mental clock as it guides you properly on time.
- Learn to respect your time as well as others' time.
- Maintain a diary of your appointments to avoid disappointments.
- Plan and organize your life properly and stay focused.
- Praise the people who are punctual as it encourages others to be punctual.
- Keep slogans everywhere such as *'Thanks for being punctual'* as it generates awareness and corrects those who don't fall in line.

Takeaways

Know the true value of time; snatch, seize, and enjoy every moment of it. No idleness, no delay, no procrastination; never put off till tomorrow what you can do today. - Chesterfield, Lord

The habit of punctuality should be developed from the childhood itself from parents and teachers. Become a role model and worthy personality to be taken seriously by others. Sometimes, a few people deliberately delay themselves to have their absence felt. It is not a good sign. Punctuality brings lot of difference in your life. Be punctual always in your life irrespective of your domain, area or sector. It pays to be punctual in this competitive world. Punctuality is the key to your success.

Quote

Thirteen virtues necessary for true success: temperance, silence, order, resolution, frugality, industry, sincerity, justice, moderation, cleanliness, tranquility, chastity, and humility. - Benjamin Franklin

KEY TERMS

- Self-improvement
- Self-esteem
- Self-discipline
- Self-motivation
- Punctuality
- Self-awareness
- Self-confidence
- Self-determination
- Self-control

BRAINSTORMING EXERCISES/ACTIVITIES

- Roll out your self-improvement plan.
- Does self-awareness have anything to do with success?
- How will you enhance your self-esteem?
- Write down few differences between confidence and over-confidence.
- Design your tools and techniques in building self-confidence.
- How do your define self-discipline?
- Jot down your strategies for self-motivation.
- Are self-control and self-mastery same?
- How can you exercise control over your mind?
- Do you think punctuality is one of the greatest habits for achieving success? If so, justify with your experiences in life.

REFERENCES

Author's Blog: <http://profmsr.blogspot.com/>

'The Power of Self-Esteem: Build It and They Will Flourish' by Jim Paterson.

3

STRATEGIES FOR YOUR SUCCESS

Six essential qualities that are the key to success: Sincerity, personal integrity, humility, courtesy, wisdom, charity. - William Menninger

LEARNING OBJECTIVES

After reading this chapter and doing the exercises, you should be able to:

- Discover the hidden leader within you.
- Realise and uncork your hidden potential.
- Write affirmations for achieving success.
- Know the techniques for dreaming big.
- Outline the tools for thinking big.
- Describe the myths and truths about hypnotism.
- Synchronise your conscious and sub-conscious mind for achieving success.
- Know the author's approach of out-of-the-box thinking *'Please don't read this....'*
- Write your goals for effective execution and achievement.

CHAPTER OUTLINE

1. Identify the leader within you
2. How to unleash your potential?
3. How to write and visualize your affirmations?
4. How to dream big?
5. How to think big?
6. How to hypnotize your mind?
7. Power of your conscious and subconscious mind
8. How to think out of the box?
9. How to unlearn, learn and relearn?
10. How to accomplish your goals?

IDENTIFY THE LEADER WITHIN YOU

Leaders don't create followers. They create more leaders. - Tom Peters

Anything about leadership inspires and excites everyone. Everybody wants to be a leader. But everybody cannot become a leader. What makes the leaders to stand out of the pack? Let us find out.

People mistake leadership is like standing in front of crowd and calling for action. In fact, it is not so what people imagine and think about leadership. Everyone is a leader if she or he influences and inspires others by setting personal example. Mother and father at home are also leaders if they play their role properly in shaping and grooming their children.

The Leader within You

A leader takes people where they want to go. A great leader takes people where they don't necessarily want to go, but ought to be. - Rosalynn Carter

Do you have what it takes to be a successful leader? Are you willing to go extra mile. Do you live for yourself or for others? If you want to live for others by serving then leadership is the next best option. Do you like to share success with others or do you like to pass on the success to others? If you want to pass on the credit of success then again leadership is the right option for you. Can you handle conflicts effectively and efficiently? Can you manage human emotions and egos properly? Can you work hard and work smart? Can you motivate and inspire others in getting the work done? Can you work in teams effectively? Can you assess the strengths and weaknesses of your subordinates and allocate the roles and responsibilities accordingly? If the answer to all the questions is yes, then you have all ingredients to become a successful leader.

Leadership Qualities

Some of the qualities of leaders are: listening, communicating, team building, visioning, trouble-shooting, negotiating, out of the box thinking, creating rather than copying, killer instinct etc.,

Leaders strongly believe in themselves. They focus more on the hard work unmindful of the results. But they are optimistic about the results. They also don't mind who gets credit for their efforts and energies. They are passionate in leading whatever the task they undertake. For them, success is only a by product not an end result. This attitude helps them to persevere and pursue their goals and objectives with persistence. In the process of leading even if they fall and fail it will not upset them as they are mentally prepared for all these eventualities. What makes them different from the followers is their tenacity and the never say die approach in achieving their goals.

Leaders have clarity of mind. They know where they are going as they are visionaries. They set their eyes beyond the reach of the common man. They may not be able to explain everything in detail to their followers. But they are basically sure of where they are going. At times, followers may be confused with the attitude and aptitude of the leaders which looks very tricky. Leaders align their followers towards the cherished goals and objectives. Whenever leaders find that the followers are off the track, they put in their efforts to get their followers on the right track and on the fast track. It is in this context, they need to inspire and motivate their followers with their effective and efficient communication skills.

Success does not go in the heads of leaders. They are emotionally balanced and have emotional intelligence. They know that overconfidence is the worst enemy. They have self-control and check themselves constantly. Whenever they make mistakes they immediately realize and correct the same through remedial action. As leaders are continuous learners, they learn a lot from their failures.

Leaders are good listeners. They listen from all sources before taking a call. They are impartial and unbiased. They see multiple perspectives and dimensions to a specific problem. Only after weighing all the options, they take the right decision. They never ignore even minor things. When followers are engrossed with problems it is the leaders who look only at the solutions and come out with a viable and feasible solutions based on their imagination and intuition.

Leadership is not a solo act. It is a process that requires interaction with others. It requires team building skills. For achieving the desired objectives, leaders have to analyze and assess the strengths and weaknesses of the members and then leverage their strengths for achieving objectives. It requires a degree of flexibility and also rigidity to form a powerful team. Mostly team building requires a lot of flexibility and in extreme cases rigidity is essential to get the team going with energy and enthusiasm.

Humility is the hallmark of leaders. They remain humble and simple however big they make. They know pretty well that success is not constant. Life is full of fluctuations with peaks and valleys. They remain cool and composed and maintain stoic silence at the time of defeat as well. Leaders know how to balance themselves well.

A leader is the one who stands by ethics. Leaders must be filled with integrity and honesty. Else they lose their credibility among their followers. Any gap between preaching and practice dents their image. Leaders need to demonstrate and stick to ethical values all the times. A person's true character is demonstrated at the time of defeat. When everything goes well anyone can be ethical and dignified. The same has to be reflected even at the time of defeat. For instance, Abraham Lincoln demonstrated his ethics and integrity when he was defeated. People are the best judges. We cannot take people for granted. Leaders are so careful about their public image, they take every care and pain when they speak something in public. It is because of Abraham Lincoln's ethical stand, people of America gave him an opportunity to become the President. Ultimately it helped America to evolve as a much more meaningful and progressive country as he endeavoured wholeheartedly for the abolition of slavery and prevented union getting disintegrated.

Leadership Training

Leaders aren't born they are made. And they are made just like anything else, through hard work. And that's the price we'll have to pay to achieve that goal, or any goal. - Vince Lombardi

Self-analysis is the key to unlock your hidden potential. First of all, find out what is your leadership style. There are several online tests, which, if executed will reveal what category of leader you are. These will also reveal your strengths and weakness so that you can overcome your weaknesses through right kind of leadership training. There are several institutes that provide training through which leadership skills can be acquired. Lot of practice is essential. No one can become a leader just by mere reading books. Books will provide adequate inputs that will serve only as guidelines. The real leadership starts only when you practice. You cannot become a crack shot unless you lose some ammunition. Only by trail and error and by practical experience people can develop leadership qualities.

Leadership is more of a skill rather than a talent. Many people believe that leaders are born. But in fact, it is not so. Leaders are made through compulsive situations. It is only the test of fire that brings out the fine steel. A smooth sea never makes you as a skillful mariner. Lot of churning takes place to get the best out of individuals. It is possible only by continuous practice. If the road to leadership were so easy then everyone would become a leader. It requires lot of struggles and sacrifices to gain acceptance as a successful leader. When we look at leaders like Abraham Lincoln, we come to know that how difficult the path to leadership was and how many trials and tribulations he underwent.

Takeaways

People underestimate their capacity for change. There is never a right time to do a difficult thing. A leader's job is to help people have vision of their potential. - John Porter

We are blessed with vast human potential. But very few people realize and utilize this potential. Successful people are smart at realizing the same judiciously and appropriately thus reaching their goals. Leadership is more of a skill rather than a talent. If hidden talents are tapped and also the requisite skills are cultivated and inculcated anything and everything is possible in this world. Sky is the limit.

Top sum up, find out the qualities required to become a successful leader. Discover your innate qualities that you possess and also the skills that you cultivated. Compare and contrast the both. Look for commonalities and align the same for achieving success. Find out what you lack and develop the same by reading, training, practice and by experience. Then you will evolve yourself as a successful leader.

HOW TO UNLEASH YOUR HIDDEN POTENTIAL?

Humanity has only scratched the surface of its real potential. -Peace Pilgrim

We are aware that all of us are blessed with certain talents and we have huge hidden potential. But very few people realize the same. What are the stumbling blocks for realizing hidden human potential? Is it because a few people think they do not possess? Or is it because even if people realize they don't persevere up to the hilt? Let us find out the same.

Self-Belief and Passion

First of all, you have to believe in yourself strongly that you have the hidden powers so that you can explore and exploit the same towards success. Having firm belief in this and being passionate will remove any obstacles that arise on the way towards success. Firm belief will tap your inner hidden energies and passion will give you kicks constantly unmindful of the results. Passion will not allow you to look at success frequently. Rather, it will drive and stay you focused on the amount of inputs. At times, being results-focused may take the people out of gear especially when people do not get results. But being passionate keep you on track thus taking you ultimately towards success.

Story of a Jailed Soldier

Once upon a time, a soldier who was caught in war was chained and arrested. He was taken to a far away island and kept in a cave with doors closed and locked. Initially, he tried to break the lock to escape. Since it was locked he could not escape. He was provided with water and limited food to survive. He tried to break the lock for a few days. But he gradually gave up his endeavors. After few days, he heard noises from outside. When he came to the door and checked it was kept unlocked. In between, the lock was removed by the people who left the island. But the jailed soldier's mind was conditioned to think that he was locked. Similarly, in our daily life, we have preconceived notions and thoughts which are difficult to be broken. Once these are broken then we can unleash the power of human mind.

Story of Closed Compartment

Ineffective people live day after day with unused potential. They experience synergy only in small, peripheral ways in their lives. But creative experiences can be produced regularly, consistently, almost daily in people's lives. It requires enormous personal security and openness and a spirit of adventure. -Stephen Covey

There is another story where Joe joined in an educational institution. He was given a cupboard which contained three separate compartments. For two compartments, keys were given to him and he opened and operated. He asked the administrative officer to provide the keys for the third compartment so that he could open and operate. He asked the administrative officer several times but the latter said that the key was with some other person who previously used the cupboard. Joe gave up asking as it was futile to ask. He somehow worked in the educational institution for a year. When he was about to leave the institution, he vacated two compartments of the cupboard and pulled the third compartment. And to his surprise it was kept unlocked. He enquired the office boy since how long it was kept unlocked. Office boy said that one day he opened the third compartment during the absence of Joe. But he forgot to inform the same to Joe and also forgot to give him the key.

Similarly, we keep our mind closed like that of the third compartment of the cupboard. By default, we develop regimented thoughts and ideas about others and behave accordingly. Only when we break the chains of conditioned thoughts and ideas, will we able to unlock our hidden potential.

Come Out of Conditioned Thinking

Everyone has inside himself a piece of good news! The good news is that you really don't know how great you can be, how much you can love, what you can accomplish, and what your potential is! - Anne Frank

Great people started from scratch. It all started with an imaginative mind. These people are not conditioned the way the majority of the people are conditioned. We have skyscrapers and great constructions. All these were achieved as they imagined and unleashed their human potential. During the course of discoveries or inventions they were treated as crazy people. Once they achieved big, people began realizing and respecting them. For instance, radio was invented by Marconi who was treated as mad by his friends as people did not understand what he was doing. Subsequently people realized what he had in his mind and respected. Opening up minds will help in unleashing the hidden potential. The problem with the majority of the people is that they don't open up and, as a result, they lie in a conditioned state of thinking.

Live in Present

You must live in the present, launch yourself on every wave, find your eternity in each moment. Fools stand on their island opportunities and look toward another land. There is no other land, there is no other life but this. - Henry David Thoreau

Research reveals that people waste 30 per cent of their precious time by thinking about the past that cannot be altered. The past worries or concerns or regrets stifles our energies and kills enthusiasm. Future is uncertain and cannot be predicted. There is no meaning in thinking about the future which is not in our hands. What we have now is only present. Therefore, always learn to live in present. Think what you would do if you were to die today. Follow the deathbed approach. When this attitude is developed then the maximum energies can be harnessed for achieving all-round success as people don't waste their precious time and energies.

You are Unique

Don't let anyone tell you that you have to be a certain way. Be unique. Be what you feel. - Melissa Etheridge

Life is a gift from the God. Everyone has a role to cut out and you were born to achieve something big in this world. Whatever you can do, you have to do in this life only. There is nothing like postponing things to the next life or birth. It is an excuse to think so. No two people are alike. Even twins are not alike. Therefore, you are unique with special talents and skills. You should learn to explore your hidden talents and exploit the skills to achieve success in your life.

Takeaways

The Bible clearly says *as a man thinketh so is he.*

Self-improvement is the key to unlock your hidden potential. Continuous learning and growing updates your knowledge, skills and abilities. From continuous learning, we begin by changing our mind, our ideas, insights and thoughts resulting into right attitude and aptitude. Therefore, you need to be a lifelong learner to unleash your hidden potential. Besides, you need to be creative and follow the road less traveled while unleashing your hidden potential so as to achieve success in your life.

HOW TO WRITE AND VISUALIZE YOUR AFFIRMATIONS?

You become what you think about most of the time. - Brian Tracy

For achieving success at any age or stage of life, it is necessary to build a strong base. It can be built by parents, social environment, educational institutions and the individuals themselves. The parents need to instill positive statements among their children to influence them at their subconscious level. The educational institutions should provide favourable climate to inculcate these qualities. The individuals have to tune their thought process through positive affirmations as they spend entire day either talking with others or through monologue. In this context, let us briefly know about affirmations.

What are Affirmations?

Any idea, plan, or purpose may be placed in the mind through repetition of thought. - Napoleon Hill

Affirmations are statements of self-talk and inner monologue that take place within the individuals from the moment they awake to going to sleep. If everything is positive then you have positive affirmations. In contrast, if you have negative thoughts then you have negative affirmations. You can become the way you want through right affirmations. Although you feed your subconscious mind regularly from your conscious mind, it is your subconscious mind which is far superior to the conscious mind. However, both your conscious and subconscious mind helps you in arriving at right affirmations.

Tools for Writing Your Affirmations

People may find it silly to write down affirmations. There is a lot of meaning in inking rather than thinking about them. Therefore, don't think but ink your affirmations. It is rightly said that a short pencil is better than a long memory. There is knack in writing affirmations. Ink them in present tense and in positive manner. Make them short, simple, straight and specific adding an emotional touch. Write your affirmations in present continuous tense rather in future tense for better results. When you do so, your faith in affirmations will be stronger as you are adding emotional and inspiring elements. You may ink like *'I am becoming great' 'I am going good', 'I am achieving big'*. Once you write your affirmations, read them daily twice - once in the morning when you wake up from sleep and again before you go to sleep.

1. Make your affirmations realistic and don't frame them on fantasy. Your affirmations should be based on dreams not daydreams.
2. Your affirmations must be credible and inspiring.
3. Connect with your affirmations to have profound impact.
4. Make your affirmations like cue cards and make them visible in your bed room and in your work place. Whenever you read you get excited and energized thus helping in getting focused on your goals and objectives.
5. Revise and rewrite your affirmations to get new excitement, if needed.
6. For effective results, make your affirmations with an emphasis on emotions, intensity, direction, motivation, persistence, repetition, self-belief, self-esteem and self-confidence.
7. As we find *'I am possible'* from *'impossible'*, we can also find *'energy in motion'* from *'emotion'* where the emotions fuel your energies and efforts and drives you towards success.

It is rightly said that a battle is won twice - first in mind and then in real life. Similarly, affirmations have to be firmly affirmed in reel life first and then in real life.

Advantages of Affirmations

The difference between success and mediocrity is all in the way you think. - Dean Francis

Affirmations build inner strength; develop inner motivation, will power, self-confidence and self-esteem. These provide emotional inputs to put best of efforts and energies to reach your goals. All successful people create their affirmations mentally while reaching their goals. Politicians, businesspersons, actors, sportspersons, teachers and students strengthen their inner beliefs and acquire knowledge through repeated self-talk about themselves. People think constantly and consciously and subconsciously when they are awake and they think subconsciously during sleep. Leveraging both conscious and subconscious mind helps in affirmations leading to success. Finally, positive affirmations provide peace, progress and prosperity for people.

Affirmations among Children

All men who have achieved great things have been great dreamers. - Orison Swett Marden

Parents should instill positive thoughts and inputs to their children. It helps them to think positively about themselves thereby becoming healthy and successful citizens in later part of their lives. Parents should be careful while feeding to their children. Children have more capacity to observation and hearing and they watch their parents closely and keenly at home. Encouraging their children to think and dream big right from childhood will help them become successful. It cultivates more internal locus of control where they start thinking firmly that their destiny is in their hands. Parents should inculcate good character and develop confidence and optimism among their children which is possible by positive affirmations.

Children are the major chunk who uses affirmations effectively. They listen to their teachers and study a lot throughout the day through constant monologue. Whatever is taught to them is reinforced through their self-talk *i.e.,* monologue. By this, they memorize the educational content and enhance their knowledge base.

How to Visualize Your Affirmations?

It's the repetition of affirmations that leads to belief. And once that belief becomes a deep conviction, things begin to happen. - Claude M. Bristol

The secret behind all successful people is visualization. This results into effective action. It is rightly said that a picture is worth a hundred words. When you visualize your affirmations pictorially with an emotional touch, you will have better results. Repeat your affirmations in a composed manner preferably in a serene place. Stand in front of the mirror daily twice and start shouting at yourself *'I am the winner'* repeatedly for a few minutes. When you hear that you are the winner you strengthen your will power as you are feeding encouraging and inspiring inputs to your mind after hearing from your sweet voice. When it is practiced regularly, no amount of cynicism and pessimism creeps in your mind. You get charged up and excited instantly. Here are a few techniques for effective visualization.

Techniques for Effective Visualization

Practice rather than preach. Make of your life an affirmation, defined by your ideals, not the negation of others. Dare to the level of your capability then go beyond to a higher level. - Alexander Haig

- Build a strong internal monologue. The moment we awake in the morning we all think till we go to sleep. This is the best way to practice our affirmations through internal monologue.
- Always thank God for what you have and similarly thank others for their help.
- Develop the attitude of gratitude. It generates positive vibes and positive thought process.
- Never doubt your affirmations. Have firm faith in your affirmations.

- During alpha state of your mind, your brain will be at its most creative and receptive state. Effectively utilize this state for better visualization.
- You can find out the attitude of the individuals the way they talk. If they talk positively, they have optimism and if they talk negatively, they have pessimism. It is all due to their internal thought process. Therefore, developing positive thought process is the key to effective visualization.
- Whenever you program your mind with affirmations at the conscious level, they will get reinforced at the subconscious level resulting into effective results. Florence Scovel Shinn rightly quotes, "You will be a failure, until you impress the subconscious with the conviction you are a success. This is done by making an affirmation which "clicks.""
- Finally, make use of all your senses such as sight, smell, sound, taste and touch and integrate them for visualizing success.

Takeaways

Success is a process, a quality of mind and way of being, an outgoing affirmation of life. - Alex Noble

Firmly affirm your affirmations for effective execution. Realise the power of inner dialogue. Don't think but ink your affirmations. Follow the techniques of writing and always think and visualize the same for achieving all-round success. Affirmations minimize negative thoughts and maximize thoughts. Life is a battle and to win the battle, affirmations would serve as an effective tool. To conclude in the words of John Addison, "You've got to win in your mind before you win in your life."

HOW TO DREAM BIG?

We all have dreams. But in order to make dreams come into reality, it takes an awful lot of determination, dedication, self-discipline, and effort. - Jesse Owens

The starting point for success in life is dreaming big. Is it possible for everyone to dream big? Yes, it is possible. But only a few people dream big and achieve success. Fundamentally, it is the dreams that take all of us towards success. But, then, why do people fail to dream big? Let us look at the same.

Failures and Dreams

The successful man will profit from his mistakes and try again in a different way. - Dale Carnegie

When people fail frequently they tend to develop mental barriers and limitations concluding that they cannot achieve anything in future. In fact, it is wrong. Every failure teaches some lessons. The positive people learn lessons from their failures and move forward. Further momentum is possible only when we restart our life with dreams. Everything is there only in our mind. We can create and conceive the mind the way we want. When our mind is fed with dreams, hopes arise resulting into investing efforts and striving for success. Therefore, it is necessary to break those mental barriers that limit from dreaming big.

Age and Ability to Dream

Children dream bigger than middle aged or old people. They live in dreams and fantasies. It is basically because they have not seen the world. They live in imaginary life. But the people in the middle and old age have seen the practical problems of life. If they happen to face frequent problems in life, their confidence level decreases. Apart from this, age does not support them to sustain their dreams. In the case of old people the ability to dream decreases further with several challenges having faced and still facing in life. There is an element of insecurity as they think that they reached fag end of their life. That is why it is rightly said, young person thinks of future, middle aged person thinks of present and old aged person thinks of past. Therefore, it can be easily concluded that the ability to dream decreases with the increase in age. However, people can dream big irrespective of age if they develop a positive mindset and they can achieve success at any age. In a nutshell, age is not a deterrent to dreaming big.

Develop A Positive Mindset

Walt Disney said. — *If you can dream it you can do it.*

It is necessary to develop a mindset that you can achieve big. When such mindset is created it is very easy to dream. Imagine that you are unique and different from others. Have firm conviction that God has created you to achieve unique things in the world. When you are flooded with such information in your mind, you get inspired and excited continuously and constantly. It develops will power, perseverance and builds confidence. As a result, you put in efforts and energies regularly which ultimately takes you towards success.

How to Dream Big?

Martin Luther King Jr. quoted, "I have a dream that my four children will one day live in a nation where they will not be judged by the color of their skin but by the content of their character." It was the dream of Martin Luther King that led to equality of blacks with whites in America. It is also rightly said that an idea with a dream can change your life.

Focus on your talents, where in, you are blessed with certain skills and abilities by birth. When you keep looking at your own strengths you tend to dream big. Few people have the habit of looking about themselves especially their weaknesses. Such tendency creates inferiority complex preventing from dreaming big. Learn to respect yourself. You must know the fact that you are unique and nobody can be like you. This kind of feeling generates positive vibes resulting into dreaming big.

Albert Einstein rightly said, "Imagination is more important than knowledge." Cultivate the habit of stretching your imaginations to unforeseen levels. Many ordinary people have become extraordinary people as they spread their wings of imagination. Imagination is essential to dreaming big. Higher the imagination, higher the dreams are. Therefore, raise your imagination levels.

So many of our dreams at first seem impossible, then they seem improbable, and then, when we summon the will, they soon become inevitable. - Christopher Reeve

Everything is possible in the world. What is needed is the will power to make it happen. Similarly, dreaming big is very much possible by giving right mental diet to your subconscious mind. Below is the process you need to follow towards dreaming big.

Half an hour before you go to bed, provide inputs to your mind that you were born to achieve something great in the world. Have conviction that you have all ingredients to achieve the same. Keep feeding your mind with such mental inputs regularly. When you think and feed your mind with the same daily just before you go to bed, your subconscious mind gets stuffed with the same. Over a period of time, your subconscious mind takes over your conscious mind and your behavior gets reflected accordingly. We do as per the instructions of our mind. When we can explore and exploit our subconscious mind in this way we tend to dream big.

Takeaways

The future belongs to those who believe in the beauty of their dreams. - Eleanor Roosevelt

Imaginations lead to dreaming big. When we dream big, our mind starts thinking big. We get excited and inspired to accomplish the impossible activities resulting into greater success. Therefore, dream, dream and dream BIG.

HOW TO THINK BIG?

I like thinking big. If you're going to be thinking anything, you might as well think big. - Donald Trump.

Thinking is a state of mind. One has to cultivate thinking big. It can happen only when you dream big. Battle is won twice, first in mind and then in reality. Unless you think big you cannot become big.

We lose nothing by thinking big. It stimulates out-of-the-box thinking, raising our aspirations and expectations. It generates positive vibes. It enhances our will power. It enhances new ways of approach. It breaks the conventional barriers and thinking.

Before you go to bed think of what you want to achieve in your life. It could be in your personal, professional or social growth. Just think big and go to bed. Do it daily. See the magic of your mind after a few days. Your subconscious mind gives you kick every time by reminding you about big things in life. You can become the way you want by thinking big. Often people do not realize the power of human mind and the magic of thinking big. Nothing is impossible in this world. Everything is possible. It is all in your mind and it is all in your thinking.

Whenever you are faced with bigger challenges in life, you start thinking bigger. Bigger problems require bigger solutions. And to get bigger solutions you need to think broadly and unconventionally. It not only enhances your mind power but also your creativity.

Tips for Thinking Big

You have to think big to be big. - Claude M. Bristol

In order to start thinking big, you need to have optimism towards life. It drives and takes you in a right direction. It constantly generates positive vibrations with in your mind to think big.

Secondly, you need to have confidence. Confidence comes from competence. And competence comes from experience. Therefore, when you have good experience it builds your skills and abilities and glides you towards life with confidence.

Thirdly, you need to surround with positive and successful people. In contrast, when you surround with negative people, they keep feeding you wrong inputs. Over a period of time, you tend to think negatively resulting into thinking small. In this context, let us take a small story.

John was passing through a forest with a goat to sell in the nearby market. Knowing this in advance, three thieves plotted to grab the goat. When John was passing through the forest, first thief met John and asked him where he was carrying the dog. John smiled and said that he was not carrying a dog but a goat to sell it in the market. After sometime, another thief met John on the way and asked him where he was carrying the dog. John surprised and said that he was not carrying dog but goat to sell it in the nearby market. As the John passed through the forest and was about to reach the nearby market the third thief came and enquired where he was carrying the dog. John now totally shocked and puzzled and said that he was not carrying a dog but a goat to sell it in the nearby market. The third thief said that he was carrying the dog but not the goat. By this time, John got vexed, fed up and began doubting and got confirmed that he was carrying the dog but not the goat. He left the goat there itself and went back to his village. Now their plan worked out and all the three thieves took the goat to market and sold it off.

From the above story, it becomes very clear about the having negative zone of people who would feed wrong inputs to change the realities. Therefore, always surround with positive and success people to think big in your life.

Fourthly, take someone who you know successful as a role model. Look at him how he achieved big and what led to his rise. Find out what is the smart work involved in reaching the tipping point. Taking such successful people as inspiration will help you think big frequently.

Fifthly, go to a serene place. Sit quietly for sometime where there is peace and tranquility. Start thinking where you want to reach. Look for all possibilities. What are the things needed to reach your goals. And start acquiring the same regularly.

Takeaways

You can do anything you want. Think for it, ask it, choose it and be committed to it. You need to break your mental barriers and limitations. Once unchained from mental barriers, anything and everything is possible in this world. Sky is the limit.

Let us all know the fact that *'to aim low'* is a crime. Let us start thinking big. It helps in the growth and prosperity of the entire mankind.

HOW TO HYPNOTIZE YOUR MIND?

The Swiss psychiatrist, Carl Jung said, *Until you make the unconscious conscious, it will direct your life and you will call it fate.*

You can achieve anything and everything in your life if you know what you want. When you can program your mind towards your goals then everything is possible in this world. Hypnotism is one of the means by which you can program your mind for success. It breaks some of the bad habits, phobias and practices that become the stumbling block towards your success. Hypnotism is all about getting your subconscious mind accept and agree to the changes you would like to make.

The word hypnotism is not new to the world. It is being practiced since many years but in different forms. It was basically used to treat illness. Franz Anton Mesmer who was an Austrian physician is considered the father of hypnosis.

When people hear about hypnotism they are scared as there are several myths and misconceptions associated with this practice. But before we look into it, let us know what the hypnotism means.

The words 'hypnosis' and 'hypnotism' both derive from the term "neuro-hypnotism" (nervous sleep) coined by the Scottish physician and surgeon James Braid around 1841 to distinguish his theory and practice from those developed by Franz Anton Mesmer and his followers ("Mesmerism" or "animal magnetism") {Wikipedia}.

"The word hypnosis is derived from the Greek word hypnos, meaning sleep.... hypnotism is a means of bringing on an artificial state of sleep to the participant ...more accurately described as a state of reduced consciousness while one is a awake {www.letusreason.org}.

Hypnosis is a mental state where in inputs are given to program mind. It is a mental state where the mind is receptive to instructions. At this stage, the mind is highly focused with concentration and yet relaxed. It is usually misunderstood as a sleeping state. It is done by an expert who is known as hypnotist on a subject.

Everyone undergoes for a state of hypnosis everyday but we do not know the same. For instance, we listen to music while going by car or when we go for a long drive, we engross into hypnosis. In fact, we all enjoy hypnosis state one way or the other.

Myths and Truths about Hypnotism

There are several myths associated with hypnotism. People looking from the background of films and hearing from unconfirmed sources, come to a conclusion that there are several dangers involved in it. In fact, it is not so.

- The myth is that the subject reveals all secrecy during hypnosis. The truth is that nothing can be revealed without the will of the subject. Only thing is that the subject discovers himself/herself during the process.
- The myth is that the hypnotist can do anything against the subject during the exercise. The truth is that nothing can be done against the will and wishes of the subject.
- Hypnotism is no way related to magic. It is purely a collection of tools and techniques involved in the process of execution.

Merits and Demerits of Hypnotism

- It helps in discovering the inner truths about you.
- It helps in improving your thought process.
- It taps your subconscious mind.
- It helps in releasing blocks, fears and phobias.
- If the right techniques are learnt you can become master of your mind by self-hypnotism.
- It helps in improving your memory which in turn helps in recalling the names and the remembering what is read. It is highly useful for all and especially for children who think that they have poor memory. Hypnotism boosts your confidence levels as well. It clearly proves that you can achieve everything in your life.
- It enhances your academic and study skills.
- It develops right mindset towards life thereby leading to success.

- It heals depression and anxiety and cures asthma.
- It helps in achieving your goals.
- Finally, it helps in taking control to become who and what you want.

Story of an Elephant

When a baby elephant was tied with a thick rope, it tried its best to break the rope. Subsequently, the thick rope was replaced by a thin rope and the baby elephant tried again to unshackle. It tried, but in vain, thinking that it was a thick rope and it could not break the rope. As the baby elephant grew big it was tied with the same thin rope. It could have easily broken it but failed to break it because of its previous failed experiments and experiences. Our minds are also programmed with several such failures and we think that it is not possible as we are conditioned like that. It is here, hypnotism helps to break such habits of failure thereby infusing fresh confidence and optimism towards life and success.

How to Hypnotize?

You must know fully about the subject thoroughly on whom it is to be practiced. Once it is known then it is easy to use the information and instructions properly to make the process effective. Ask the subject to lie down, allow him/her to relax. Ask him/her to close his/her eyes then encourage the subject to take a few deep breaths. The objective of this entire exercise is to clear the clutter from the mind of the subject for desired outcome. Later on, use the tools and techniques depending upon the requirements of the hypnotism. For instance, if you want to enhance the memory of the subject then use the relevant techniques for the same. Similarly, if the subject has certain phobias then use appropriate techniques accordingly. The procedure is same but the instructions depend on the type of problem to be addressed. The hypnotist must be an expert to avoid any negative fallout.

There should not be any disturbances during hypnotism as it can break concentration. Sounds arising out of phone, telephone, radio beeper or any other things should be avoided. The place of hypnotism should be totally serene for desired results.

Takeaways

Hypnotism, if used properly, you can get desired results. It is a proven technique where you can make use of it for achieving success in your life. Once you learn the tricks of the trade then you can try on yourself as well as on others. Lot of practice is needed in this regard. Finally, you need to have right attitude towards hypnotism to leverage benefits for all-round progress, growth and success.

POWER OF YOUR CONSCIOUS AND SUBCONSCIOUS MIND

Whatever the mind of man can conceive and believe, it can achieve. Thoughts are things! And powerful things at that, when mixed with definiteness of purpose, and burning desire, can be translated into riches. -Napoleon Hill

Human mind has two parts — conscious and subconscious mind. Both play a crucial role for functioning of human mind. The conscious mind is voluntary that you are aware and it goes by logic, analysis and reasoning. In contrast, the subconscious mind is involuntary. It is not known to you and you are unaware. It contains emotions, heart beat and breathing rate. When you look at your loved ones your emotions rise, heart beat increases. It happens due to your subconscious mind.

People with high emotions go by heart rather than the reasoning of mind. Especially when someone loves deeply, he does not go by any reasoning or logic. He just follows as he is emotionally attached with the opposite sex.

You can heal your disease through the power of your mind. It is your mind responsible for most of the illness. When you can conquer your mind then you can conquer your disease almost one-third.

Although subconscious mind is programmed from conscious mind, it is superior as it is the place for emotions and imagination. The motivational levels of people start from here only. Subconscious mind is like a magnet that immediately and instantly attracts the ideas that have emotional content. If you want to break your old habits you have to touch your subconscious mind first, then only it is easier to unlearn and learn. Unfortunately, most people fail to program their minds properly. The research from neuroscience reveals that subconscious mind controls 95 per cent of our daily activities.

People take decisions based on intuition and gut feeling which is nothing but taking decisions based on their subconscious mind. The conscious mind works with logic, analysis and perceptions. The subconscious mind is well framed and programmed from the inputs received from conscious mind. For instance, when someone hits a person, the latter immediately either defends or offends. It is basically because the persons reciprocates from his/her subconscious mind spontaneously. Simultaneously the conscious mind thinks of what to do next in the given situation.

During waking hours, the conscious mind works. While in sleeping hours, the subconscious mind comes to the fore. For instance, Anne was a housewife. She had the ability of instructing her subconscious mind when to wake up early in the morning. She never set clock but told herself firmly the time to get up. Her husband was so surprised over her programming the subconscious mind. She had the ability to influence her subconscious mind strongly. Anne was an alarm clock by herself. It indicates the power of subconscious mind.

When you learn new things your conscious mind will be fully alert. As the time passes, you get used to these things. That means your subconscious mind takes over in charge from your conscious mind. Your subconscious mind is like an autopilot.

The thoughts and the beliefs that you have in conscious mind will be transferred to subconscious mind automatically. For instance, if you sow right seeds in your conscious mind, you reap right plants in your subconscious mind. If you feed your mind with good thoughts that you can achieve everything in your life, the same will go to your subconscious mind. In a nutshell, the conscious mind is the creator while the subconscious mind is the executor.

Diana and David

The interpretation of dreams is the royal road to a knowledge of the unconscious activities of the mind. - Simone Weil

David and Diana worked in a same place. Diana was the senior most as she had been working in the company for the last 6 years. David was older to Diana with higher experience in other companies.

But he was the junior most in the organisation. As per the organisational requirements, David had to work with Diana until he got grooved and groomed with in the system.

David initially hesitated to work with Diana who was younger but respected her intellectual and educational background and started working together. Diana was a polite and well mannered. She was bold and beautiful. She was a woman of principles and values. David began liking her behavior and worked together for six months. David began thinking deeply about Susan. He always took the positive aspects of Diana although a few commented that Diana was stubborn and a trouble maker for getting the things done. Since David was an independent thinker he began thinking of his own and started feeding positive information and inputs about Diana to his subconscious mind. Over a period of time, David began thinking deeply about her all the time and even in his dreams. Later on, David realized that he began loving Diana.

From the above story it becomes very clear about the importance of feeding subconscious mind with right inputs. If David fed wrong inputs about Diana in his subconscious mind, he would have developed hatred against her. Therefore, everything depends on how you think and how you program your subconscious mind. Never ignore the power of your subconscious mind.

Synchronize your Conscious and Subconscious Mind for Success

You are the most powerful magnet in the universe! You contain a magnetic power within you that is more powerful than anything in this world, and this unfathomable magnetic power is emitted through your thoughts.
- Rhonda Byrne

Common people do not know the power of both conscious and subconscious mind. Only success people know the significance of both and leverage them. When there is right harmony between the both, there can be peace and success. When people feed themselves with negative thoughts, they end up with negative results. Right inputs will lead to right outputs. When you program your mind with healthy and progressive thoughts regularly, over a period of time, you can achieve the desired changes in your life with your subconscious mind.

The subconscious mind is like an obedient soldier who obeys the instructions from the conscious mind. It does not know the difference between good and bad. Whatever the orders passed by the conscious mind will be obeyed and executed. Therefore, make sure that your conscious mind gives the right orders to your subconscious mind.

The subconscious mind can be compared with a vehicle which runs as per the directions of the driver. If your subconscious mind is a puppet then your conscious mind is the puppeteer. Therefore, learn to pull the strings effectively and efficiently for achieving all round success.

When teacher explains the subject repeatedly it goes deep within the subconscious mind of the students. Since subconscious mind does not go by logic and analysis, it goes purely by repetitive instructions. If students have to understand effectively then the teacher has to focus on key things repetitively. It is for these reasons; great speakers repeat the key ideas, points, and thoughts in different ways and means to get across the message.

Takeaways

The subconscious mind makes no distinction between constructive and destructive thought impulses. It works with the material we feed it, through our thought impulses. The sub-conscious mind will translate into reality a thought driven by fear, just as readily as it will translate into reality a thought driven by courage or faith. - Napoleon Hill

You can be what you are if you can shape your subconscious mind through right commands from your conscious mind. Only with limited usage of our mind power we achieve many things. Imagine the amazing results when you can reap by using your mind fully. Do how many people put in their efforts to explore their mind power? It is only a few. Those who succeed in life are the people who know how to utilize their mind power fully.

Always dream big. When you dream big then imagination comes from your subconscious mind. When your dream is strong you will definitely achieve. Focus more on the strength of your dreams. When your strength of dreams is stronger then the reality of success would be sure and certain.

HOW TO THINK OUT-OF-THE BOX?

Great minds discuss ideas; Average minds discuss events; Small minds discuss people - Eleanor Roosevelt

Whenever people are confronted with several problems they brood over on the problems rather than looking at the solutions. A few people look at the problems and find a few solutions and opt for the best one. And there is another set of people; they look at the problems from different multiple perspectives unconventionally and come out with viable and feasible solutions. When they think in novel and unconventional we may call it as out of the box thinking. In a nut shell, "Out of the box thinking" can be defined the process of thinking multiples solutions for a given problem by coming out of conventional constraints and barriers. The concept originated from USA in late 1960s and early 1970s and several management experts are involved in evolving this concept.

'Out of the box thinking' is basically status quo ante. It is mostly possible for trailblazers who leave a mark behind. Those who think outside the box are creative people and are basically ideas and solutions oriented people. They have the extraordinary ability to generate multiples solutions for each problem. They are non-traditional and unconventional thinkers. Many inventions are the result of out of the box thinking.

Please Don't Read This

The author wrote a case study titled *"Please Don't Read This…Prof.M.S.Rao"* and posted in his Blog. It was an interesting case study and helps people to think and analyze the case study. It contained emotions, feelings, egos and hidden and unexpressed love between two personalities (Refs http://profmr. blogspot.com/2009/03/please-dont-read-this-profmsroa.html). Usually when people are asked to read, they may not read. But when they were asked not to read then they started reading and there was an overwhelming response to the post with cross section of people offering their comments. It was an instant hit. It was possible as the author thought unconventionally and created curiosity among the readers to visit his Blog and read.

Dhirubhai Ambani

When we look at Indian businesses, Dhirubhai Ambani rose from ranks and established Reliance Empire by adopting unconventional methods during license raj. There were too many controls for doing business in those days in India. But he explored unconventional ways and means to promote business and became a successful entrepreneur. He started the equity cult in India which helped his business to grow as well as the Indian investors. He taught Indian investors about the share market business and encouraged them to explore investments in this area. He brought investor education and awareness. All this was possible through *'out of the box thinking'*. Whenever people are faced with stumbling blocks they convert the same into building blocks through creative methods.

Competition and Creativity

Creativity is inventing, experimenting, growing, taking risks, breaking rules, making mistakes, and having fun. - Mary Lou Cook

The business world is beset with cut throat competition and to beat the competition, companies are trying to innovate themselves with new features, products and services. Although people say that competition is a bane, but, in business world it is treated as a boon as it keeps the companies moving forward with creativity and innovation. Companies try to offer products, services with more features for lesser, cheaper and faster ways and means. It ultimately benefits the consumers. The *'out of the box'* methods and unconventional business strategies will help stay ahead of competition thereby adding value to consumers.

Mahatma Gandhi's Unconventional Leadership

When the entire world was beset with attaining independence through violence, Mahatma Gandhi came up with the tenets of truth and non-violence for attaining India's independence. Everyone doubted the competency and relevance of these principles as people believed in the principle of *'might is right'*. Finally, Mahatma Gandhi led to India's independence through non-conventional methods successfully. Martin Luther King applied the same to bring equal rights for black along with whites. Leaders often believe in *'thinking out of the box'*. They rarely follow the crowd. They rather follow where there is no path thus leaving a mark behind.

Susan and Ron

Ron and Susan worked in a similar department in an organisation. Ron and Susan gelled with each other as they have several commonalities. Ron was extrovert, with energy and enthusiasm. Susan was introvert and a woman with strong character. She was bold and beautiful. She was a very cool, composed and charismatic woman. He enjoyed talking with Susan often. And Susan also liked the company of Ron. Gradually they developed mutual admiration for each other. Both Ron and Susan usually did not interact with other colleagues unless there was need for any official communication. Other colleagues in the office were surprised with these two people gelling with each other. There were two women colleagues who were jealous with the amicable relations and they began giving negative inputs about Susan to Ron. Ron was basically an independent and original thinker and could smell the negative intentions and kept away from these two negative women.

Since the plan did not work out, these two women kept on giving negative inputs about Ron to Susan. Over a period of time, Susan stopped talking with Ron and the latter felt that something went wrong with former. Ron guessed that this might be the work of these two negative colleagues.

He tried to meet Susan number of times to persuade about the situation so that she would not get trapped by these two negative women. Unfortunately, Susan maintained more distance with Ron.

Ron was basically a man with perseverance, persistence and passion. He was passionate about Susan and tried number of times to reach her. He looked for several conventional solutions to reach her, but failed such as personal visit to convince, email communication and through telephonic conversation. At last, Ron thought unconventionally for this problem and succeeded in reaching and persuading Susan. People give up addressing the problems after having tried one or two solutions. But the people with perseverance will find number of solutions for solving a single problem just because they never give up.

Both Ron and Susan reconnected with each other and gelled with each other. Later on, both expressed their love towards each other and finally married and lived happily. When love is true and strong, nobody can break the relations.

Ron as a Researcher

Ron joined in a research organisation for developing books related to HR subjects. When he joined the firm there was number of books already released from the shelves of the research organisation. He found it difficult to create books as there should not be any overlap of books on the same topic. Therefore, he entered into the domain of leadership development where there were limited books released. After entering into the domain, he found that there were number of styles and theories on leadership. He explored fully and looked for areas where there were research gaps. He probed and researched in that domain and developed books on specialized styles and theories of leadership. What Ron did was to travel the unconventional path where no one traveled in the past thus becoming a trailblazer in the domain of leadership development.

Tools for Unconventional Thinking

It is better to have enough ideas for some of them to be wrong, than to be always right by having no ideas at all.
- Edward de Bono

- You need to come outside your comfort zone to think unconventionally.
- To be creative, follow a different route map to reach your office as it leads to thinking in a new direction.
- You may take any item and start thinking about its application and utility in multiple ways. Don't be content if you get one or two ideas. Keep exploring in multiple ways. You will be amazed to know that you will get more creative over a period of time.
- You must be willing to take risks and tread the path to uncertainty and complexity.
- Open up your mind, be a good listener and be receptive to new ideas.
- No idea is too small to be ignored. You must learn the fact that an idea can change your life.
- Develop observation skills as it throws light on new things. Many people do not observe well resulting into ignorance. When we listen to the story of Sir Issac Newton sitting under an apple tree, he observed the apple falling on the ground due to gravity. And he suddenly thought of the Universal Law of Gravitation.
- Go to a serene place and start thinking, you will develop new ideas which you never imagined.

Individuals need not to be intelligent to think unconventionally. Out-of the box thinking requires thinking skills which even average individuals possess. When they can think in different directions they develop several permutations and combinations resulting into creative solutions.

Takeaways

One of the advantages of being disorderly is that one is constantly making exciting discoveries. - A. A. Milne

In this cut throat competitive and complex world we need to be creative. We need to be different from others to stay ahead of times; else we will be lost out in the race. Get out of your conventional constraints. Remove your mental barriers and limitations. Fortune favors only the brave. The world is only meant for brave hearted not fainthearted. Therefore, dare to be different but don't be indifferent.

HOW TO UNLEARN, LEARN AND RELEARN?

The illiterate of the 21st century will not be those who cannot read and write, but those who cannot learn, unlearn, and relearn. - Alvin Toffler

Learning is a continuous process from cradle to grave. It widens your mental horizons, changes the perceptions and expands your overall intellectual base. According to Stephen R Covey, one of the seven habits of highly effective people is learning, that too, continuous learning. Continuous learning is an exercise to your mind as physical exercise is to your body. To be successful in life, it is necessary to focus on physical, intellectual and spiritual learning.

Continuous learning keeps you updated with latest developments. It changes your mindset with the changing times. It sheds some of your old inhibitions, hesitations and habits. It helps you in reinventing yourself constantly.

Continuous Learning

View life as a continuous learning experience. - Denis Waitley

Let us appreciate the fact that everything starts small. It is human nature, where in, none becomes great in overnight. It requires lot of energies and efforts regularly. Everyone has to start small somewhere. Therefore, there is need for learning on a daily basis. The learning need not be by books alone as many think. Learning includes by way of observation, reading, experimentation, practice, training etc., usually people learn by reading books. There are many people with little literacy achieved success, learning by their observation and trial and error method. If learning is the end, the means are many. Whatever the constructive means individuals adopt, finally, it should lead to healthy learning.

Case study of Cohen

The real voyage of discovery consists not in seeking new lands, but in seeing with new eyes. - Marcel Proust

Cohen worked in an industry for 25 years. He decided to share his knowledge, experience and expertise with student community. Therefore, he joined as a faculty in an engineering college. Having worked for 25 years in the industry, he found it very difficult to get along within the educational institution initially. But his passion to teach students compelled him to unlearn some of the habits which were not required for the educational institution. He was basically ruthless as a manager and leader in the industry. He was highly task oriented and aggressive in nature. But the educational institution needs lot of patience to handle students. In addition, lot of reading is necessary to teach. He struggled a lot to recall his olden days where he prepared for his academic examinations. He had to prepare more than what he prepared during his student life.

But the passion towards teaching made him to prepare long hours. He prepared notes by himself by referring number of books. Gradually he began developing his own content with several examples so that students would understand easily. It took around three months to unlearn some of his industry habits and learnt new tools and techniques towards teaching. Thorough reading and passion made Cohen to unlearn, learn and relearn several things to become a successful faculty member. Cohen also innovated his own way of teaching methodologies by blending both his industry experience with academic experience. Ultimately, he became a successful faculty member by unlearning, learning and relearning.

Age and Ego for Learning

Learning is a treasure that will follow its owner everywhere. - Chinese Proverb

For learning, ego and age should not be a hurdle. We can learn from anybody whether they are older or younger to us. What is important is to recognize that the other person has certain competencies, skills and abilities and probably people lack. Knowledge can be acquired by respecting others' potential. Some people hesitate to consult people younger to them as their ego prevents them. Such filters within mind should be eliminated. There was a person by name, John, who joined in a research company. He had 23 years of experience in the industry but was new to the research company. He had huge appetite for learning and growing. He did not hesitate to learn the ropes of the research from younger people. Finally he rose in the research department within a short time as he was not egoistic in consulting and learning from younger people. He combined his previous experience with the existing knowledge and ultimately outsmarted others in the research firm with in a short span. What is needed is to block the ego, which, in most of the times is a stumbling block for learning.

Tips to Unlearn, Learn and Relearn

The ink of the scholar is more sacred than the blood of the martyr. - Mohammed

Have a firm and flexible mindset set that you are still learning and evolving. Don't take your learning for granted. The learning that takes place during your life may subject to change. The globe was initially believed to be flat. But the subsequent learning confirmed that the globe is round. Therefore, have a flexible and open mindset towards learning.

Try to associate with intellectual friends. You can share your knowledge with them. As well as you can learn. Probably, you may have some of the ideas which are unconfirmed. Creating intellectual ambience can lead to confirmed learning. In addition, it creates more knowledge base. When you discuss with them, the hidden potential within you will surface and you may share the same with them. When others challenge your ideas, then also, you tend to think deeper resulting into creativity and innovation.

Mentoring will help you to communicate effectively. It also helps you to explore and examine your mentees. It is a two way communication where you can share your knowledge, expertise and experience. Besides, you can be benefited from the practical experiences and learning of your mentees. Apart from guiding, grooming and gliding your mentees towards their career success, you can get cross checked about your knowledge from their experiences. If there are any variations, the same can be unlearnt and learnt.

Take continuous feedback from your well-wishers and experienced people. Constructive feedback helps in taking the right steps for remedial action for improvement. If there are any deviations in learning, the same can be unlearnt. In this process, care should be taken to consult the right experts who are the authority on the topic.

Finally, be passionate in the process of unlearning, learning and relearning. The passion has to come from the core of your heart.

Takeaways

Live as if you were to die tomorrow. Learn as if you were to live forever. - Mahatma Gandhi

People need to have open mind towards learning. Many students think that once they complete their academic education, their learning is over. In fact, the real learning starts from the moment they enter into employment. The basic educational qualifications are only the launching pad for getting employment. The real survival and success in the organisation front is possible only by unlearning, learning and relearning with the changing times.

HOW TO ACCOMPLISH YOUR GOALS?

The world makes way for the man who knows where he is going. - Ralph Waldo Emerson.

What is Goal Setting?

Every human being has an inherent, innate urge to grow and get recognition. It is natural trait amongst all the human beings to do something unique and extraordinary in order to get noticed. It is because of this urge, man invented many things right from the Stone Age and evolved himself as the most intelligent animal that can talk, memorize and reason. All the latest technology, comforts, innovations and inventions etc., are the result of the root desire to excel and get noticed from the crowd. Although all human beings are gifted with many qualities and traits, it is only a few who explore their inherent strengths and succeed in the society. And the majority gets absorbed in the crowd. Goal setting is a tool since time immemorial. The people those who succeeded from Stone Age to space age have set their goals one way or the other.

Goal setting is an interesting tool and, if used as the right technique, man can succeed in his life. The management books emphasize this as it has become a vital for the success of any institution or organisation. Goal setting has been added in the educational curriculum to stay positive, constructive, focused and results-oriented.

Significance

Everyone has a goal either directly or indirectly and whether one pursues seriously or casually and whether knowing it consciously or unconsciously. Goal setting as a tool can unlock the vast hidden human potential. Harvey Mackay quoted, "Goals give you more than a reason to get up in the morning; they are an incentive to keep you going all day. Goals tend to tap the deeper resources and draw the best out of life".

Goal setting as an idea can change the world within you and around you. It makes an individual to plan properly. It provides a sense of direction and prepares to organize properly. It constantly awakens an individual to remain alert both physically and mentally. It builds up confidence and competency. It raises the levels of energy and enthusiasm. It cultivates passion and it brings out the best from the people. In addition, it helps in managing one's time efficiently and effectively.

Types of Goals

Goals vary from person to person depending upon the values one cherishes. For example, the goal of Mahatma Gandhi was to attain independence for our country from British. The goal of a sportsman is to win medals in Olympics. The role of a businessman is to stand number one in his/her business line. The goal of a student is to stand first in his/her class or to stand first among all institutions. Likewise goals differ from individual to individual depending upon their tastes and temperaments.

However, the goals are basically divided into short term and long term goals. Again, the span of long term and short term differs from context to context. Usually less than a year, it is known as short-term goal and if it is more than a year, it is known as long term goal. People need to have both short term and long term goals and these two must be closely related. To emphasize on the significance of long term goals Charles C. Noble rightly said, "You must have long term goals to keep you from being frustrated by short term failures".

For instance, when people want to become successful businesspersons, they must set their short term goals in such a way that the successes or achievements made out of the short term goals must be intertwined with their long term goals. Even if there are short falls or set backs resulting out of short-term goals, the long-term goal will not be lost sight of as it was aptly said by Charles C. Noble.

In marketing language, goals are known as targets and the marketing people continuously strive to reach their marketing targets. By this way also the companies expand their business.

Jack Welch of General Electric (GE) highlighted about stretch goals. When the goals are stretched, people work with more dedication, determination and discipline. Because stretching oneself leads to touching upper limits and touching one's upper limits bring a great sense of fulfillment and satisfaction. One way the stretch goals are encouraging and enlightening and force an individual to stretch to greater limits.

How to Set Your Goals?

Abraham Lincoln said, "A goal properly set is half way reached". First, find out your strengths and weaknesses and list out. It is desirable to consult your trusted colleagues to assist you in this exercise. All human beings have biases and prejudices. If assessed by yourself it may not give you correct analysis. Acquire the correct analysis and report of your strengths and weaknesses. After listing out your strengths in the assets side and weaknesses in the liability side, you can deeply analyze and can come to a conclusion about your personality profile. Then you list out your inner ambitions and goals whether they are matching with your profile. Whether these are achievable and reachable and what are all the obstacles or hindrances or the stumbling blocks on the way to reach the same. It is a typical mental exercise but once the process is completed it is almost like a winning half of the battle.

All efforts must be made very clear to see that the goals are not conflicting and contradicting with each other. Check whether your goals are in tune with your principles, policies, philosophy and ideals. If found to be in tune than go ahead. It is like what Epictetus said, "First say to yourself what you would be; and then do what you have to do". The next stage is to break the goals into smaller parts or elements. You can also divide the goals into short term and long-term goals. Here another important thing is to commit your goals on paper. Some one rightly said, "Write it down. Written goals have a way of transforming wishes into wants; can't into cans; dreams into plans; and plans into reality. Don't just think it - ink it! " Studies revealed that 95 percent of the people don't write their goals and it is only 5 per cent write and their success rate is higher.

After classifying written goals into short term and long term goals, break down the tasks further on a daily, weekly, fortnightly, monthly, quarterly and annual based. By executing in this way you will get focused and it becomes easier for you to monitor your performance periodically. It is like a few people making annual resolutions on every New Year day and tracking the same at the end of the calendar year.

Goals should be set in such a way that you must be able to work with passion rather than under compulsion. While setting the goals there should not be any influence from parental side, family side or friends' side. And don't set the same goals, which others have set and succeeded, as goals will vary from person to person based on attitude and aptitude. In a nutshell, don't copy others' goals.

While setting goals, usually set small, achievable, and reachable goals. Any effort to set bigger goals in the initial stage itself will lead to failure and demotivation thus upsetting the apple cart. Global steel giant Mr.Lakhsmi Niwas Mittal said, "Set realistic and achievable goals. After achieving the same, set further higher goals". For each goal there should be a deadline and fixed time frame. Ensure that the goals have multi-utility purposes and objectives. At times intuition can prove handy in setting goals.

It is rightly said, "A successful person doesn't quit trying once a goal is reached, but sets a new one and keeps going". Always reward yourself after reaching each small goal. It boosts your energy levels and also serves as a motivational tool.

Goal Setting for Students

Students should recognize their inner and inherent abilities in the childhood itself. A goal, which is focused for a long time and that too from the tender age itself, will become more meaningful and realistic. "Goals are discovered, not made", said Richard J. Foster. In this context, the parents must play a pivotal role to find out the hidden talents of their children by scientific or psychometric analysis tests and must nurture the children. Simultaneously, teachers have also a vital role to play in this context. They are also involved in shaping the minds of the students. If the approach is triangular *i.e.*, from parental, teacher and student level then the probability of reaching goals faster and quicker are brighter.

Goal to Become a Civil Servant

If a student dreams of becoming an IAS (Indian Administrative Service which is a prestigious civil servant post in India), s/he should get equipped right from the elementary school level itself.

For this, there should be both short term and long term goals. In short term goals, the student should stand out academically by reading the entire subjects voraciously from different dimensions. The student must be a good leader in the school level itself by organizing various social and cultural activities. S/he must excel in all types of competition such as quizzes, essay writing, extempore speech etc. The student must also participate in sports and extra curricular activities, which builds qualities like team spirit, camaraderie, killer instinct, organizing ability and sociability. Like wise, the student must be all rounder right from the school level to university level. Succinctly the student must be jack of all domains and master of a particular domain.

The short-term goals, which the student achieved, will indirectly correlate to his/her long-term goals of becoming a prestigious civil servant. The extracurricular activities like reading newspaper daily, winning in essay writing, extempore speeches; debates will groom the student to become an eligible participant for civil services. The student is sure to succeed in the competition examinations and will come out with flying colors because s/he knows something of everything and everything of something. Such a wonderful example of a particular career is given to effectively combine both short-term goals and long term goals chronologically and systematically in order to make it like a case study for all students aspiring to become a civil servant.

Goal Setting in India

Although goal setting is a universal thing, there will be difference in analysis and application of this tool from one country to country because of diversified cultural, social, political and economical backgrounds. In the case of India, goal setting is based on herd mentality/instinct, and it is mostly dictated and directed by parental wishes and guidance. Rather to put in a nutshell, goal setting is not based on aptitude but on attitude. Once upon a time, becoming an IAS/APS was considered respectable and commendable. Many students showed their eagerness to get into these services because of the prestige and power associated and attached to it. Gradually things changed the other way round with the changing times, technology, tastes and temperaments.

Indians are basically strong at mathematics and now they are strong at Information Technology. Students began concentrating on professional qualifications like engineering, medicine and management. These days everyone wants to become an engineer or doctor or a management executive. It is basically because to get fat pay and perks, to get placements faster and to get settled quicker with comforts. So we can conclude that Indian culture of goal setting is purely based on herd instinct. Parents also want the quick settlement of their children in their lives.

Why Do People Fail?

The shortest way to do many things is to do only one thing at a time", quoted Sydney Smiles. People fix too many goals at a time and confuse themselves. The so-called multitasking is not effective in goal setting, as the individual is not able to focus on a singular activity with concentration. Such things lead to confusion and chaos resulting in failures. Besides, it is a known fact that failure rarely stimulates positive vibes except in case of a few extraordinary individuals.

Some people are good starters but are poor finishers. They start with a bang and end with a whimper. When they are faced with obstacles their initial enthusiasm gets fizzled out thereby neglecting their goals. Overconfidence is the worst enemy. People tend to rate themselves as superior humans and take everything for granted resulting into failures. Some people are a confused lot and they keep changing their goals frequently resulting in a fiasco. Lack of involvement and resources could result in giving up goals.

Setting unrealistic goals could prove to be counter productive. People often fail to break a big goal into small elements and make futile efforts to achieve and fail miserably. Lack of sincere and sustained efforts may be another reason. "Vision without action is a day dream, action without vision is a nightmare", goes the Japanese proverb. In few cases people work without any proper planning resulting into a fiasco. People often confuse between hard work and smart work. In fact what is needed is the combination of hard work and smart work that can deliver healthy and positive goods to reach goals. Improper time management is one of the key reasons to failures.

Procrastination is the thief of time. People are in the habit of postponing the difficult tasks resulting into procrastination. Once the goal is set there has to be determination to reach by any means. In some cases, people do not organize actively towards their goals due to lethargy. In this context Elbert Hubrard clearly said, "Many people fail in life, not for lack of ability or brains or even courage but simply because they have never organized their energies around a goal".

Obstacles to Goal Setting

The American author, Dale Carnegie said that man had to conquer six types of fears - fear of criticism, fear of failure, fear of old age, fear of poverty, fear of ill health and fear of death. It is fundamentally both the fear of failure and fear of criticism that are the stumbling blocks to goal accomplishment. People tend to worry and they fail to retry after their repeated failures. One should make a note that success is the product of successive failures.

Wavering mind is the worst enemy of a man. Once the goal is fixed the mind should not waver from goals. People, at times, get engaged with too many other activities and lose focus from goals. Lack of emotional support either from family or friends can divert the attention. Inadequate resources may become another obstacle. People are often faced with internal and external threats. In most of the cases, the internal threats can be managed. In contrast, the external threats can not be managed effectively which are, in fact, beyond human control. If they are sidetracked temporarily they must be in a position to place themselves rightly on the track mentally. Things like insecurity, at times, become another major mental block.

Tools and Techniques for Accomplishment

Always develop the ability and capability to hit the bulls' eye. Periodically monitor and review your goals. Whenever you reach your goals, try to reward yourself with a small break or holiday or a gift which drives your energy level to the higher level. Regularly check yourself whether you are sidetracked or sidelined from your committed or chosen path. Set reminders to cross check whether you are on the fast track.

Daily read the written goals once in the early morning when you get up from your bed and again when you go to bed. By doing so, your goals will automatically go to your subconscious mind which will serve as a reminder whenever your mind goes out of sight or out of the way of your chosen goals. Try to come out from your comfort zone and enter into effective zone, which brings thrill and joy and keeps you going. Always attempt to touch your upper limits. Once you reached a goal, set tougher goals so that you tend to touch your upper limits further.

Try to motivate and hypnotize your mind and visualize that you have reached your goals. Treasure mapping and visualization work as wonderful tools to reach your destination. Close your eyes for some time, visualize the success and then open your eyes, you will find yourself with radiating energy and enthusiasm. It refreshes and recharges your mind.

Daily allocate fixed amount of time for your both short and long term goals. Try to remove your psychological and mental blocks and myths, which hinder your path. Create a friend circle that contributes towards your goals and values either directly or indirectly. Collaborate your different goals into one and streamline rather than indulging in conflicting, confrontational and competing goals.

You should always be guided with single objective, which must be highly focused. In the Hindu epic - Mahabharat, the teacher Dronacharya was often blamed by his students who belong to the faction of Kauravas and especially Duryodan that he was showing partiality to Arjun of Pandava faction. The teacher Dronacharya who was vexed with frequent allegations by Duryodan offered a test to showcase the skills what Arjun possessed. Dronacharya arranged a fish, which was kept hanging with a thread with in a tree and asked all his students to tell what they saw in the tree. Everyone could not notice the fish and said that they found leaves and fruits. But it was only Arjun who said to his teacher (Dronacharya) that he was able to see an eye (*i.e.*, eye of a fish). It shows that Arjun was highly focussed on his goal (*i.e.*, eye of a fish) not even the fish. Then Dronacharya told his students that all his students were equal but it was Arjun who was more dedicated, concentrated and focused on his goals. Therefore, you must stay focused on your goals and that is the mantra of success and the secret of success.

Wherever it is possible, simplify your life by removing complexities. Be committed and do not say 'yes' to all other unrelated tasks for the sake of courtesy as such things will divert and divest you of your objectives. Try to keep motivational and inspirational postures related to your goal at your home and at your work places. Listen to the audio CDs related to your goals and watch video CDs that will elevate you. Always think, dream and sleep with your goals and one day, you would find that you have reached your goals and the entire world applauding over your achievements.

Takeaways

The road from nowhere to number one is not easy and it is an uphill task. It requires a lot of planning, organizing, directing, and preparation, controlling both internal and external deviations, which might sidetrack or sideline the cherished goals. Materially, motivationally and managerially, it requires a confluence of various factors and resources. In this context, Aristotle aptly said, "First, have a definite, clear practical ideal; a goal, an objective. Second, have the necessary means to achieve your ends, wisdom, money, materials, and methods. Third, adjust all your means to that end."

You should accept goal setting as a strategy and adopt it as a powerful tool and technique. Set your goals rightly, get into the correct track, follow the right track and be always on the fast tract to reach your beloved and cherished goals.

M.S.R. Goals

Jim Collins - 'Good to Great' gave a tip to have Big, Hairy, Audacious Goals.

Goals must be (M) motivational and inspirational. The goals so set must move you constantly on your toes. It must provide daily fuel to your body and mind and energize with enthusiasm. Arnold H.Glasgow rightly said, "Make your life a mission – not an intermission". Your life must be filled with energetic activity with a mission to achieve your goals.

Make your goals (S) simulating and stimulating. The goals will make you to visualize your success in simulated conditions. Such simulated mental success will raise your interest to achieve your goals in realistic world.

When you set (R) reachable and realizable goals, there will be a higher success rate to accomplish your goals. When you set feasible goals it enhances confidence to move ahead with optimism and dynamism.

MESSAGE

Never change your goals. Setting goals is like setting your destination towards success. If required, change only your strategies to reach your destination but not the destination itself, however problematic the path towards your destination might be. Madam Curie won Noble prize twice. She said that path to success was not easy. She always worked against all odds and reached her goals successfully.

Remember the wonderful words of Ursula K. Leguin, "It is good to have an end to journey, but it is the journey that matters in the end".

KEY TERMS

- Leadership
- Affirmations
- Hypnotism
- Out-of-the-box thinking
- Human Potential
- Visualisation
- Conscious and Subconscious mind
- Goal setting

BRAINSTORMING EXERCISES/ACTIVITIES:

- Can you identify leader within you? If yes, jot down the same.
- Mention briefly qualities required to become a leader.
- Write briefly whether leaders are born or made with examples.
- Write your affirmations and find out the ways to fulfill.
- What are the techniques of writing affirmations?
- Is age deterrent to dreaming big? Illustrate with examples.
- Think of ways to enhance your memory through hypnotism.
- Illustrate few ways of thinking out of the box.

REFERENCES

Author's Blog: <http://profmsr.blogspot.com>

<http://www.wendi.com/html/what_is_hypnosis.html>

<http://en.wikipedia.org/wiki/Hypnosis>

<http://www.letusreason.org/Nam3.htm>

www.letusreason.org <http://www.letusreason.org>

<http://profmsr.blogspot.com/2009/03/please-dont-read-this-profmsrao.html>

4

SUTRAS FOR YOUR SUCCESS

Don't get complacent. Push yourself out of your comfort zone and set higher standards of achievement for yourself. Once you've achieved a standard of excellence, never let it rest—push yourself even higher. - Dave Anderson

LEARNING OBJECTIVES

After reading this chapter and doing the exercises, you should be able to:

- Develop killer instinct.
- Know the process of team building.
- Practice humility.
- Appreciate the importance of networking skills.
- Describe common skills.
- Understand the importance of NLP for better personality.
- Learn the principles of communication.
- Comprehend body language better.
- Understand how mentoring helps you in evolving as a successful person.

CHAPTER OUTLINE

1. Is killer instinct essential for success?
2. How to build successful team?
3. Humility is the hallmark of great leaders
4. How to develop networking skills?
5. Common skills,
6. NLP
7. Communication skills,
8. What is body language?

9. Assertiveness
10. Mentoring myths and truths

IS KILLER INSTINCT ESSENTIAL FOR SUCCESS?

To achieve admiration and respect today, the warrior must set himself apart from the rest of society by his personal excellence. Where warriorship was once a birthright, it is now a calling. —Living the Martial Way

What is Killer Instinct?

I live on my gut instinct. - Melanie Brown

Killer instinct is a strong will to win and an urge to succeed unmindful of the consequences for others. It is a fighting spirit. It is not flight but fight to the finish. It is demonstrates *'do or die'* scenario. It is a combative and competitive mentality to win at any cost.

The killer instinct is confluence of courage, confidence, competence, fortitude, resilience and tenacity. It is combination of physical, mental and spiritual powers. Doing something even if the odds are insurmountable requires killer instinct. It is like having guts to try again whether you succeed or fail. It is like exploring the unknown without any fear of failure. At the same time, killer instinct does not mean being ferocious and careless in your approach. It outlines calculated strategy to maximize efficiency, effectiveness and safety.

How to Develop Killer Instinct?

I usually go with the first instinct, and then build upon that. - John Otto

To develop killer instinct, people should shed some of their old habits. In military organizations, soldiers are trained to shed unwarranted habits and practices so that they can evolve themselves as successful and competent combatants. Therefore, it is obvious that killer instinct can be taught through right ambience and training. Killer instinct is a mindset that can be cultivated and inculcated.

- Always be in the effective zone not in the comfort zone.
- Know your strengths and weaknesses and also your opponent's weaknesses.
- Don't be overconfident as overconfidence is the worst enemy.
- Don't be unduly sentimental and emotional. Strike a right balance and maintain composure with maturity.
- Be passionate in your chosen area of interest.
- Always be cool and composed.
- Avoid both internal and external distractions and stay focused on your goals.

Characteristics of Killer Instinct

Ideas pull the trigger, but instinct loads the gun. - Don Marquis

Here are a few characteristics of killer instinct such as cool and composed thinking, physical and mental intelligence, fortitude, courage, gut feeling and intuition, ability to anticipate others' strategy, resilience and tenacity, being always in effective zone rather than in comfort zone.

Takeaways

And so you touch this limit, something happens and you suddenly can go a little bit further. With your mind power, your determination, your instinct, and the experience as well, you can fly very high. - Ayrton Senna

Killer instinct is a quality we all need whether in life or in work. It helps in conquering the unknown. It will make you nose in the face of difficulty and set out to accomplish your dreams even if it means facing the risk of failure. Although killer instinct is an innate trait but people can cultivate a few skills and abilities that collectively give rise to killer instinct. We find entrepreneurs, sportspersons, soldiers and leaders across various sections achieving success by leading from front with killer instinct.

It is a well admitted fact that we all have killer instinct but the intensity varies from person to person. There is no doubt that killer instinct is essential for achieving success in your life. Therefore, demonstrate your killer instinct and come out with flying colors in all your endeavors.

HOW TO BUILD SUCCESSFUL TEAMS?

Coming together is a beginning. Keeping together is progress. Working together is success. - Henry Ford

With the rapid changing technology, there is growing need to work in teams to leverage the benefits at the workplace. The companies insist people with flair for working in teams. Those who are social and amicable with fair degree of flexibility and adaptability can become successful team members. Team building is a challenging task and it is always easier said than done. Although everyone knows the importance of working in teams individuals often tend to work independently as they have fear of losing their importance and getting their hard work unrecognized. Rather individuals often have apprehensions of somebody hijacking the fruits of their energies and efforts.

What is a Team?

T.E.A.M = Together everyone achieves more. - Author unknown.

Team building is process of planning, organizing, influencing, staffing, directing and motivating the members with a common objective of reaching organizational goals and objectives. Organizations are looking at the individuals who can work in teams as the projects cannot be handled by a single individual. The present day corporate environment calls for working in teams to reach the set objectives. It is an active process where people of divergent tastes and temperaments come together to work under a common objective. The two letter word *'we'* rather than the one letter world *'I'* is the hallmark of teams. Managing teams is indeed a Herculean task.

Importance of Teams

None of us is as smart as all of us. - Ken Blanchard

There are several advantages in team building such as:

- Teamwork makes ordinary people as extraordinary people.
- It promotes relations among the members by minimizing any misunderstandings and by maximizing productivity and performance through cooperation, coordination and open communication.

- It unlocks the hidden potential of the participating members.
- Team members can bring their varied experiences and expertise to the team building process and the same can be integrated effectively and efficiently for achieving organizational goals and objectives. It will help in having better takeaways. When they go elsewhere for building teams, the same takeaways can be utilized thereby enhancing both the individual and institutional growth.
- Team members learn a lot through team participation as they learn to respect others' ideas and insights thus widening their knowledge base.
- Above all, there is fun and joy by working in teams.

Process of Team Building

No one can whistle a symphony. It takes an orchestra to play it. - H.E. Luccock

Select a team leader who has flair for leadership and team building. Once the right team leader is selected, give free hand to select the team members as per the vision of the company. Build trust among the members by setting personal example. Communicate openly and lay a mission through which the vision can be executed. Allocate the roles and responsibilities based on their strengths and weaknesses. Provide full support to the team members. Whenever they have doubts, clarify and motivate them. In case of non-cooperation among the people find out what bugs them. Emphasize on commonalities rather than differences. Educate about the importance of working in teams and motivate them. Whenever the problems arise always focus on solutions rather than brooding over problems. Encourage risk taking among the team members. Respect failures while execution of the tasks and implore them to learn lessons out of their mistakes and keep moving ahead. Throughout the entire process of team building, ensure that the activities of the team members are aligned with the vision of the company. Offer constructive feedback for their improvement and betterment. Encourage creativity and innovation whenever they are faced with problems. Above all, set personal example by participating actively into the team building process.

There are professional team building consultants and facilitators who can be hired for building effective teams in organizations. They play a pivotal role in assessing the needs of the teams and offers suggestions. It is always advisable to hire these professionals outside the organizations who find out the flaws existing within the teams for providing remedial action. Asking the team building consultants and facilitators within the organization may lead to organizational prejudices which defeat the very purpose of team building.

Tips for Team Building

The ratio of We's to I's is the best indicator of the development of a team. - Lewis B. Ergen

Given below are the few tips for team building.

1. Team builder or leader should know that everyone is unique in nature, abilities and capabilities and adds value in their own way. Realizing this makes the process of team building easier.
2. Clarity of mind of the team builder plays a crucial role in building effective teams.
3. Build trust. Create a favourable environment.
4. Develop emotional intelligence and promote soft skills among members.

5. There has to be an open communication, coordination and collaboration among the team members. At times, little bit of competition should be encouraged among the team members tc stir up their minds and to add dynamism and energy.
6. Minimize micromanagement. Micromanagement is a process where the superior involves in close observation and supervision of subordinates. Give adequate freedom to team members to work on their own way and at the same time supervise them.
7. Break the barriers and build bridges.
8. Look for commonalities not differences.
9. Make connections from person to person, mind to mind and heart to heart.
10. The team builder or leader should not have any personal prejudices towards any of the team members.
11. Encourage by giving incentives to the individuals volunteering for team activities.
12. Thank the people who always support the team activities.

Takeaways

No man will make a great leader who wants to do it all himself, or to get all the credit for doing it. - Andrew Carnegie

If communication is the sister of leadership then team building is the brother of leadership. Team building is always easier said than done as it is challenging to manage human egos, emotions and feelings. Stephen R. Covey emphasized the significance of teams in his book *'The Seven Habits of Highly Effective People'*. One of the habits of successful people in the world is working in teams. Therefore, people need to develop the mindset to work in teams to reap benefits for themselves as well as for their organizations.

HUMILITY IS THE HALLMARK OF GREAT LEADERS:

I believe the first test of a truly great man is his humility. I do not mean by humility, doubt of his own power, or hesitation in speaking his opinions; but a right understanding of the relation between what he can do and say, and the rest of the world's saying and doings. - John Ruskin, Modern Painters (1843)

When there is storm the strongest and biggest trees get uprooted but a simple grass survives by changing its direction in tune with the storm and comes back to normal position after the storm goes away. The tree is very strong with its roots and not in a position to change its direction. As a result, it gets uprooted. But a simple grass changes its direction through its flexibility and survives from storm. In fact, the simple grass stands taller than a tree. It demonstrates its humility and survives successfully from storm. The people those who are successful in the world have one of the greatest virtues i.e. humility.

What is Humility?

Humility does not mean thinking less of yourself than of other people, nor does it mean having a low opinion of your own gifts. It means freedom from thinking about yourself at all. - William Temple

People often think assertiveness either as aggressiveness or submissiveness although it does not mean the same. Similarly humility is neither inferiority nor superiority complex. It is neither submissiveness nor aggressiveness. It is neither undervaluing oneself nor overvaluing oneself. It is neither talking low of oneself nor blowing one's trumpet. To put it succinctly in the words of Charles Haddon Spurgeon, "Humility is to make a right estimate of one's self."

Humility is all about modesty. People often confuse between humility with timidity. Both are poles apart. Humility is all against pride while timidity is absence of courage. Humility is admitting that you don't know everything and asking others for help. You must be able to consult and seek help from your subordinates, or peers who are experts in a particular area. It is treating others with respect without any arrogance. It is about listening to others. It is being courteous with others whether you need help or not. It is also about allowing the wrong doers to save their face in the presence of all. Humility is the hallmark of great people and it is one of the greatest virtues of all.

True Vs False Humility

True merit, like a river, the deeper it is, the less noise it makes. - Edward Frederick Halifax

When people submit so as to gain something from others by way of promotions, perks, or recognition, we may call such behavior as false humility. However, when people demonstrate their simplicity and humility through thick and thin without expecting anything in return we may call such behavior as true humility. Therefore, both true and false humility are poles apart and it is always the true humility that alone triumphs in the world.

Advantages of Humility

We come nearest to the great when we are great in humility. - Rabindranath Tagore

There are endless advantages with humility. You can expect friendly and warm relations from others thus improving your relations with others. You can command respect from everyone. It presents and projects you in a positive light in front of others. It minimizes anxiety and maximizes performance at the workplace. It eliminates the conflicts arising out of ego clashes. The pleasure you get out of humility is truly immense.

Leaders with Humility

To become truly great, one has to stand with people, not above them. - Marleen

Charles de Montesquieu

One of the greatest traits of great leaders is their humility. It keeps leaders rise above the rest. It makes them totally different and distinct from others. It requires humility to accept failures. It requires humility to give credit to the deserving people rather than swallowing. In case of a failure, a good leader says, *"We have failed because of my mistake"*. In case of a success a good leader says, *"We have succeeded because of the efforts of our team"*. It requires not only courage but also humility to accept the debacles and failures. To put it in the words of Eisenhower, "A sense of humility is a quality I have observed in every leader whom I have deeply admired. I have seen Winston Churchill with humble tears of gratitude on his cheeks as he thanked people for their help to Britain and the Allied cause. My own conviction is that every leader should have enough humility to accept, publicly, the responsibility for the mistakes of the subordinates he has himself selected and, likewise, to give them credit, publicly, for their triumphs."

Jim Collins in his Level 5 leadership mentions that the leader should have both professional will and personal humility. It becomes obvious that one of the key ingredients of leadership is extreme humility. The level 5 leaders are so passionate about their goals that they don't mind who get credit for their efforts and energies. They are karma yogis. Jesus Christ, Mahatma Gandhi, Martin Luther King and Mother Teresa, to name a few, are indeed the leaders with great humility. They may belong to different spectrum but they stand unique, different and tall from others because of their humility. At times, leaders remain as unsung heroes due to their humility.

How to Practice Humility?

Wash out your ego every once in a while, as cleanliness is next to godliness not just in body but in humility as well. - Abbe Yeux-verdi

- Solitude is fortitude. Go to a serene place where there are no external distractions or disturbances. Analyze yourself. Find out your strengths and weaknesses. Look at the ways and means to overcome your weaknesses.
- Practice fasting. Fasting not only cleans the internal system but also enhances inner energies and iron will to become strong and humble.
- Go for meditation. Meditation is the best method of realizing oneself without any external influence. It makes one to think about oneself honestly and helps in bringing the desired changes.
- Always be humble to your superiors, be courtesy with your peers and be kind to your subordinates. This attitude will transform you as a humble person over a period of time.
- Be a karma yogi. Do your duty. Don't expect rewards for your efforts. Let people judge what you are.
- Remember the slogan, 'Empty vessels make much noise'. Speak less and listen more. The more you listen to others the more you learn and respect others' knowledge and ideas. It reminds you of the right place you actually belong vis-à-vis others resulting into behavioral changes for refinement and improvement.
- Continuous feedback is essential to know where you stand. Take the feedback honestly without any false ego. It helps you assess yourself how far you are reaching towards humility.

Takeaways

Humility is the solid foundation of all virtues. - Confucius

Humility is a virtue found in the great people. When people achieve one success after another they become more humble. Humility is also possible as one gets older. The humility index goes up when you reach higher positions.

We can learn through the lives of great leaders about the humility. The common thread connecting across all great leaders irrespective of their areas of interest in the world is humility.

Humility is a learned skill. It is essential for everyone to cultivate this skill for gaining acceptance with others and for achieving all round success in life and for making a difference to the world.

HOW TO DEVELOP NETWORKING SKILLS

If you build a network, you will have a bridge to wherever you want to go.- Harvey Mackay

Do you want a career of your choice? Do you want to get your contract executed successfully? Do you want to get noticed as a leader in your domain? Do you want to help others? Do you want to rise above from the rest? Networking is the only mantra for all these questions.

What are Networking Skills?

It's all about people. It's about networking and being nice to people and not burning any bridges. — Mike Davidson

In this complex and competitive world, to be successful in life, you require both hard work and network. Networking skills are all about being good with others and being helpful to others without expecting anything in return from them. Networking is about sharing knowledge, information, ideas and insights that build everlasting relationship. Aristotle said that man is a social animal. He cannot live alone. He needs people to socialize and move forward. Abraham Maslow, in his hierarchy of needs highlighted about the importance of social needs once both physiological and security needs are met. All these things prove beyond doubt about human beings craving for socialization and affiliation. Networking is subset of socialization wherein all the involved parties can leverage mileage for their mutual progress and prosperity. It is like clapping with both hands for achieving all round success.

Qualities of Networkers

The networkers have to go an extra mile. They need to possess several characteristics such as being open, receptive, flexible and winsome. They should be good at attentive and active listening skills. They must be able to memorize the names of the people to become close to them and may have to go out of the way to help others. It is an added advantage if they have magnetic personality to attract and network with others. Succinctly, they should think of how much they can give rather than how much they can take from others. Above all, they should have the attitude of gratitude.

Merits

The successful networkers I know, the ones receiving tons of referrals and feeling truly happy about themselves, continually put the other person's needs ahead of their own. – Bob Burg

Some people have magnetic personality and they attract people and network easily through their charisma. And some people hone these skills. These skills are essential everywhere be it in business, career for achieving all round success. It helps in unwinding ourselves. It also helps in getting to know and appreciate others' areas of interest.

It helps in survival and success. If you have sound networking you can get the things done by telephonic conversation alone. It helps in getting employment as it is reported that 85% of the jobs are available through networking alone. The concept is known as referral recruitment where the presently working employees of a specific organization refer the people known to them to their employers. It minimizes the costs involved in conducting an interview for employers as well as getting the best talent in a shortest possible time.

How to Develop Networking Skills?

Prepare a list of like minded people irrespective of your industry. Meet them personally and regularly, if possible. If it is not possible, call them over phone and enquire about their well being.

Join in Clubs or associations or forums where you will have better influence and can get noticed. Of course, it is also essential to network with people outside your domain as well. Spend your quality time with people with whom you gel well. Retain the network you already have. It is two-way traffic. As you need two hands to clap you also need to reciprocate with response from others without any expectation and anticipation. Below are few tips for effective networking skills.

- Always be winsome.
- Give a firm handshake when you meet people.
- Maintain eye contact.
- Listen attentively.
- Encourage people to talk.
- Find similarities not differences.
- Maintain a separate diary of contact numbers and addresses for future and further follow-up.
- Display natural enthusiasm and energy while interacting with new people.
- Send mails to them on occasions of their birthday or something special that touches them.
- Learn to remember the names and important events about the individuals.
- Strengthen what you have and gradually expand for new links. Don't lose diamonds when you are in search of stones.
- Be genuine and don't be phony.
- Build bridges not barriers.

Takeaways

Networking is an essential part of building wealth. — Armstrong Williams

In this uncertain and complex world we need to secure ourselves which is possible only through right networking skills. It is a kind of insurance to protect our future by helping and seeking help from others. What goes around will come back to us. Maintain contacts regularly without expecting anything in return. Don't hesitate to help as well as to seek help so as to grow successfully in your personal, professional and social life.

COMMON SKILLS

People may have heard of soft skills and hard skills. Perhaps very few people may have heard of Common Skills. Let us look at these skills.

We talk about common sense in daily life. That means the common qualities, which are expected out of human beings, based on a particular cultural background. When people make silly and folly mistakes, which are not expected out of them, we usually question *'Don't you have common sense?'* Likewise, common skills are the skills and abilities, which are connecting and running through a common thread that are fundamentally essential for the survival and success of the people. These skills become the core skills for human beings and we can call them as core skills or key skills. Since these skills ensure survival and success of the people we may call them as survival skills and success skills. There are plenty of common skills but let us briefly take TEN key skills, which are common.

Ten Common Skills

Communication skill: Communication skill is the key of all skills. We all communicate from womb to tomb. Man can not survive without communication. He communicates either by verbal language or by non-verbal language or by the combination of both. The ability and the skill to receive and reciprocate one's feelings and emotions by all these elements is known as communication skill.

Creativity: All individuals must possess the ability to create and recreate. Many inventions have surfaced because of this ability. Individuals should not only learn the things but also be able to create new things based on their learning and observation. And for all this, creativity becomes again another core skill.

Career development: Managing and developing one's own career is essential so as to survive and succeed in life. There could be many personal, social and professional compulsions. When one is able to develop one's career, naturally there will be all round development of personality.

Team spirit: Ability to work in teams is necessary. When people learn to develop team spirit by working in teams, the results can be faster and smarter. If numerically one plus one is two, in team spirit one plus one is more than two because of the synergy in strength.

Technology: This is the world of technology where technology is dominating the world. Not knowing or not learning technology may lead to many complications and implications. People should know the basics of technology and should equally know the application of the same. For instance, now-a-days, Internet has become common thing. If people know how to make use of the minimum computer technology they will know how to survive and succeed better.

Time management: Although rapid changes in technology have brought many comforts, it has made life more complicated and complex. People do not find time and it is often heard every where that *'I don't have time'*. God gifted us with 24 hours of time a day. Every one should know how to manage time effectively and efficiently. Setting priorities by categorizing as A, B, C, D & E can prove to be beneficial. A stand for the most important activities which if not addressed will have far-reaching negative implications. B stands for important activities and if not executed will have minor negative fall out. C stands for the activities, which have to be addressed but not having any significance. D stands for the activities, which can be addressed if time permits. And last but not the least is the E, which stands for insignificant activity. If addressed it is okay or else it can be sent to trash. So setting priorities can save time, energy and precious resources.

Sociability: Aristotle aptly said, 'Man is a social animal'. Man can't live alone; he strives for affiliation and social acceptance. A few people found to be socially inept. In such case, it becomes a liability. For the success and survival of the people it is essential to develop the trait of sociability. Therefore, this skill becomes the core skill and one of the fundamental features of the common skills.

Self-development: People should learn to manage and develop themselves. It is inherent quality hidden in all human beings to grow. Every one wants to grow from birth to death in all faculties. Only when one develops oneself one can develop others. Therefore, managing and developing of oneself becomes a core skill.

Numerical ability: It is essential to have knowledge of numerical ability. Having numerical bent of mind is essential in daily life. Not only having this ability but also to have the ability to apply, as well in the real world is necessary.

Problem solving: World Health Organisation (WHO) has made problem solving as the 8th life skill. Everyone confronts problems from birth to death. Problems are part of life and every problem, at times, leads to an opportunity. Man becomes tough only when he faces problems because every problem teaches some lessons in life. 'A smooth sea never made a skillful mariner' goes the saying. In fact when the going gets tough the tough gets going. Hence the problem solving becomes the tenth most crucial skill amongst all common skills.

There are number of other skills which belong and become the part of common skills. For instance, cognitive skill *i.e.,* the ability to think creatively, critically and analytically is the one. Empathy - that means the ability to get into the shoes of other person and think. Research *i.e.,* the ability to go in depth in a field or activity for creating base for further and future studies. Personality development and likewise the list of common skills go on in length.

Correlation of Common Skills with Soft and Hard Skills

People do get confused with common skills, hard skills and soft skills. There are both thin and thick lines that separate all these three concepts. Soft skills are the skills that are essential for the survival at the corporate world that enhances employability. Anything other than domain knowledge is also known as soft skill. These are also known as people skills and Emotional Intelligence. Soft skills are specialized skills at the work place more on a professional plane. Where as the common skills are the key skills, which are simple skills, related to personal and social life. The hard skills are just the domain knowledge and are related to the subjective knowledge. Hard skills deal with 5 W's such as What, Why, Which, Where and When. The soft skills deal with 1H *i.e.* How? If what you have become the hard skills, how you present the same becomes the soft skills. All the three skills are interrelated and if interwoven makes an individual highly successful personality.

Takeaways

What common sense is to human sense, the common skills are to human skills. Both hard and soft skills can be compared with two layers of the earth with lower layer being hard skills, surface layer being soft skills. And deep within the core of the earth being the common skills. And also common skills are known as core skills which become the infrastructure, then hard skills are known as domain skills which become the superstructure and finally the soft skills are known as surface skills which become the superior structure.

NLP (NEURO-LINGUISTIC PROGRAMMING)

"To be a good communicator, you need 3 things. First, to know what outcome you want.

Second, you need maximum flexibility in your own behavior. Third, you need to be able to notice, fully and accurately, the responses you are getting?" (<http://www.gp-training.net/training/communication_skills/nlp/quotes_nlp.htm>)

Now-a-day, there is frequent discussion about Neuro-Linguistic Programming (NLP) across the world. Let us know what is all about NLP and its advantages.

NLP is all about cognition, communication and change. It also focuses on self-awareness, attitude, personality development and psychology. It indicates the relationship between brain, body and language. It was developed by Richard Bandler and John Grinder in 1970s aimed at human excellence. It is widely used by several professionals for helping their customers and clients. Given below are the two definitions about NLP.

Co Founder Richard Bandler and John La Valle explain Neuro-Linguistic Programming as :

Neuro: The Nervous System through which experience is received and processed through the five senses.

Linguistic: Language and nonverbal communication systems through which neural representations are coded, ordered and give meaning.

Programming: The ability to organise or communication and neurological systems to achieve specific desired results. (<http://www.ppimk.com/NLP/NLP-What.html>)

NLP, or Neuro-Linguistic Programming, is the study of human excellence and communication. It provides us with the tools to run our own brain and manage our states, emotions and behaviours. (<http://www.thecoachinginstitute.com.au/what-is-nlp.html>)

Merits

- NLP helps in your self discovery and enhances personality development as you will have better awareness about yourself.
- NLP practitioners and trainers use this tool to bring out the best from the participants by enabling them to realize properly resulting into better communication and behavior.
- It helps you in becoming what you want by changing your thinking.
- It helps you to think better thereby improving your learning skills as well as social and soft skills.
- It helps you to align your goals effectively and efficiently.
- It builds you optimism and confidence which are essential for all-round personality development.
- It not only promotes communication skills but also team building and leadership skills that are essential for professional success.
- It promotes listening and observation skills thus helping to find the hidden data in any communication.
- Through NLP techniques, you will be in a position to influence your audience through communication by gauging and analyzing their body language. It helps you to become a successful public speaker.

NLP techniques are widely used in several sectors for reaping rewards. There are several trainers and practitioners to execute this instrument. It is advisable for students to get trained in NLP so that they can develop and evolve themselves as successful professionals.

COMMUNICATION SKILLS

The ability or the skill to transfer one's thoughts, ideas and information from the sender to the receiver with the latter being understood the same effectively and efficiently is known as communication skills. It is one of the greatest skills of the soft skills and its importance is growing rapidly due to the rising complexities as a result of technological inventions.

In corporate terminology, communication is the process of exchange of information from the sender to the receiver and vice versa. There are different types of communication such as downward communication, upward communication, horizontal communication, crosswise communication, verbal communication; written communication etc., In downward communication, the flow of information is from the people at the superior level to the people at the subordinate level. On the other hand, in upward communication, the flow of information is from the subordinate level to the superior level. In horizontal information, the flow of information is from the people of same level to that of their counterparts at the same level. In crosswise communication, the flow of information is from one level to any other level which is either diagonal or crosswise without any reporting relationship. In verbal communication, the flow of communication, which is transferred orally to any level, and it is the most effective one as one can communicate effectively with one's body language so as to have profound impact on the receiver. Whenever, there is a need to record the information in black and white, and then people go for written communication in which the communication is through mass mailing in written form.

Any communication has seven elements, apart from the noise, which is known as the barrier in communication and also can be treated as the eight element of communication. The first element being the thought or an idea, the second is encoding the same, third is the transmission of the message or the channel, fourth being the reception of the message and the decoding the same is the fifth element, understanding of the decoded idea or thought is the sixth element and the last and final element i.e. seventh element is the feedback of the receiver to the sender as a sign of confirmation of the communication. Any effective communication must possess the seven elements and the communication is complete with the combination of these seven elements. In case, if there is any gap between the sender and receiver or vice versa then there is communication gap or miscommunication or which is technically called as noise. The so called eighth element is the culprit of communication and all efforts must be made to eliminate it.

Every leader or manager must have great command over communication skills as communication takes major portion of time in any organization. It is aptly said, 'Communication is the life blood of an organization'. It is through communication all people are connected in the organization and all the activities are coordinated to achieve their goals and objectives.

The media of communication is divided into verbal communication and non-verbal communication. Both the oral and written communication falls in the fold of verbal communication. The non-verbal communication is divided into body language and sign language and the latter is further divided into visual signs and audio signs. As it is quite obvious, oral communication is the exchange of ideas, thoughts and information in oral form and if it is in written mode, it is known as written communication. A person must be strong at both oral and written forms. When an individual work in the capacity of a manager he will be required to give presentations frequently and he must be in a position to deliver the same effectively. Similarly, he may be asked to write reports on various projects or tasks and possession of written communication is sine quo non.

It is said that 93 per cent of our communication belongs to non-verbal language. In contains both voice modulation and body language. The oral language is always supported by body language and there has to be consistency in both oral and body language, otherwise, it will give rise to credibility crisis. For instance, when an autocratic manager of an industry talks about the application of participative type of management hereafter by thumping his desk physically with force is an indication of inconsistency in his body language with that of his oral language. In a nutshell, our body language conveys our true intentions unconsciously although we may consciously speak orally different. Body movements and gestures contain 55 per cent, voice tone and inflection contains 38 per cent and the combination of the both is 93 per cent, which conveys our non-verbal language. While the rest 7 per cent belongs to verbal communication. The combination of all the percentages becomes 100 per cent which becomes the media of communication.

Characteristics of an Effective Communicator

- He must be very clear in his mind what he wants to convey so as to reach the audience effectively.
- The language must be simple, straight and should hit the bull's eye. It is the quality not the quantity of the message that counts.
- He must demonstrate his confidence by way of his body language and must radiate energy and enthusiasm so as to create positive impact in the minds of the receivers.
- He must assess the maturity level of the audience and must communicate accordingly.
- He must not use loaded language with phrases or complicated terminology or jargon to avoid confusion.
- He must organize his mind properly with thorough preparation and enough home work to make it reachable and everlasting.
- All out sincere efforts are to be made to prevent barriers in communication.
- There should be total consistency in his verbal and body language.
- Should adjust his tone level as per the message of his speech, with pauses and emphasis wherever it is essential.
- Must have ability to raise the curiosity level of the audience.

All efforts must be made to enhance the quality of communication from time to time with innovative methods and approaches. For instance, Swami Vivekananda referred the audience at the Chicago conference as the brothers and sisters of the world, which is still memorable even today. He was a great communicator and speaker.

Communication skill is one of the top ten soft skills without which soft skills are irrelevant. Those who are qualified in their academics and try for placement, the interviewing officer emphasizes more on this ability. A weak communicator creates problems for himself and for others. The interviewing officer can not afford to take a risk by accommodating a poor communicator. Good communication is a feature of effective personality development. Those who want to succeed in their careers; it is imperative to possess good communication skills.

WHAT IS BODY LANGUAGE?

The body never lies and the body never keeps quiet. — Ancient Chinese proverb.

Observe the three role playing activities stated below:

One: Peter says, "Paul, take this DVD cassette. It is very interesting. Play it and enjoy yourself". (Not looked at the DVD and also at the Paul while handing over).

Two: Peter says, "Paul, take this DVD cassette. It is very interesting. Play it and enjoy yourself". (Looked at the DVD but not looked at the Paul while handing over).

Three: Peter says, "Paul, take this DVD cassette. It is very interesting. Play it and enjoy yourself". (Looked at the DVD, maintained eye contact with Paul and smiled while handing over).

From the above three role playing activities it is obvious that the third activity is the best as the Peter smiled, looked at the DVD and maintained eye contact with the Paul. It is obvious from the above the huge signification and importance attached to the body language during communication. In this context, let us know in detail about the body language.

What is Body Language?

When we communicate only 7 per cent of the communication depends on verbal communication and the rest goes towards the non verbal communication. Of the 93 per cent- 38 per cent is voice modulation and 55 per cent is body language. It indicates the tremendous impact it makes during communication. Body language constitutes the total facial animation and body animation. Human beings may say many lies but it is the body language that usually speaks truth. When we communicate the other person observes and registers our body language in his subconscious mind. Although externally, the listener observes and accepts everything of verbal language but the listener's subconscious mind is totally beset with our body language.

Interpretation of Body Animation

Non Verbal Behavior Interpretation	
Standing with hands on hips	Readiness, aggression
Sitting with legs crossed, foot kicking slightly	Boredom
Sitting, legs apart	Open, relaxed
Brisk, erect talk	Confidence
Arms crossed on chest	Defensiveness
Walking with hands in pockets, shoulders hunched	Dejection
Hand to cheek	Evaluation, thinking
Rubbing the eye	Doubt, disbelief
Touching, slightly rubbing nose	Rejection, doubt, lying
Locked ankles	Apprehension
Hands clasped behind back	Anger, frustration, Apprehension
Head resting in hand, eyes downcast	Boredom
Rubbing hands	Anticipation
Sitting with hands clasped behind head, legs crossed	Confidence, superiority
Open palm	Sincerity, openness, innocence
Tapping or drumming fingers	Impatience
Pinching bridge of nose, eyes closed	Negative evaluation
Steepling fingers	Authoritative

Patting/fondling hair	Lack of self-confidence, Insecurity
Titled head	Interest
Stroking chin	Trying to make a decision
Pulling or tugging at ear	Indecision
Biting nails	Insecurity, nervousness
Looking down, face turned away	Disbelief

Tips for Better Body Language

Below mentioned are the common tips for effective body language and the same varies from culture to culture.

- First and foremost thing is to be aware of your own body language and capitalize the same effectively and efficiently.
- "The eyes are the windows, the mirrors of the soul", goes the Chinese proverb. The use of eyes in the process of communication is called Oculesics. Maintain eye contact to the listener. And do not stare at the listener as it creates inconvenience and discomfort for the individual. If you find it difficult to look into the eyes then look in between both the eyes, it appears as though you maintain eye contact.
- Keep your back straight but not stiff and don't slouch your body. You may slightly tilt your head forward to demonstrate your interest.
- Don't stand still in a place. Make a few comfortable movements with in your personal space.
- Proxemics: This refers to the way in which people maintain a physical distance from one another. Learn to maintain the right gap between intimate and public zone. Intimate zone is the zone for well known and close people. Where as the public zone is meant for unknown people. Never offend others by entering their personal zones during conversation or communication.
- While shaking hands be confident and positive and ensure that your palm should neither by upwards nor downwards but just be equal and vertical as it conveys assertive approach.
- Smile from the core of your heart. People are intelligent and can make out whether the smile is genuine or fake.
- Make use of your hand movements up to the hilt. Each verbal language must be consistently correlated to have effective delivery of speech.
- Observe the film stars and great speakers across the globe closely for correct body language. Try to implement the same as per your convenience, comfort and that suits your culture.
- Look into the mirror and speak, you can make out if there are any inaccuracies in your body language because you are the best judge for yourself.
- Deliver any speech in the presence of your friends and family members and ask them to bring to your notice for evaluation and correction.
- Visualization technique proves to be useful while delivering any speech. Visualize your role model vis-à-vis body language and adopt the same. Over a period of time you can develop positive body language.

- Videotape your conversation, communication or your speech and then check by muting the recording. By this, your body language can be observed fully and the areas that need to be improved can be corrected and adopted.
- Never view body language in isolation. It has to be seen keeping the cultural context view.

Takeaways

Body language is the most crucial part of any communication. Fine tuning body language helps ordinary persons to become an extraordinary persons thereby excelling in all walks of life. Improving your body language can make a big difference in your people skills, emotional intelligence, attractiveness and general mood. The difference between the good leaders and great leaders is the right application of body language to convey, enthuse and inspire their followers.

ASSERTIVENESS

Assertiveness is the art, ability and the knack of saying 'No' without hurting the rights of others. It is an average of aggressiveness and submissiveness. It is one of the core ingredients of soft skills. Below are a few tips for asserting yourself.

Tips

- State your feeling properly, positively and firmly without hurting others.
- Always empathize with others by being a good listener. Listening to others properly paves the way for better understanding of their view points resulting into assertive communication.
- Be objective, specific and clear in your approach.
- Be cool and composed and never lose your temper. Know the fact that it takes years to build the relations but it takes seconds to break the same.
- Present positive body language to present your viewpoint.
- You can go for sandwich conversation wherein you start positive initially then add your strong points to put across and finally end the conversation with positive so that other person carries the message properly.
- When you dislike the actions of other person, instead of saying *'you did like that'* you may say that *'I did not like that'*. Although the message is same there is feeling of *'I'* which defuses the problem subtly.
- Always think of the ways and means to assert yourself.
- Keep repeating your points firmly till the message goes strongly to the other person.
- Never say 'Yes' to unfair and unreasonable requests.
- Practice assertion skills during the free time through your internal dialogue.
- Do meditation regularly as it helps your thoughts and emotions under control and helps for assertiveness in the long run.
- Take feedback from your trusted friends about your behavior for bringing out desirable changes.
- Never think of win-lose or lose-win but always think of win-win situation.

The above mentioned tips will help you to succeed in all walks of life.

MENTORING-MYTHS AND TRUTHS

We make a living by what we get; we make a life by what we give. - Winston Churchill

Do you want to survive for a day or live for a life time or to be remembered for generations in the history of mankind? If your goal is to live longer and larger than life by becoming a priceless and timeless person then mentoring is the right option.

What is Mentoring?

Mentoring is a brain to pick, an ear to listen, and a push in the right direction. - John Crosby.

Mentoring is a powerful empowerment tool where both mentor and mentee grow personally and professionally. It is the process where the mentee's investments are direct and mentor's investments are indirect. Mentoring takes place in informal environment. It helps in transferring knowledge, skills, abilities and competencies from mentor to mentee. It requires good understanding and synergy between the both. It involves more of learning than teaching.

It is a type of partnership where sharing of experiences takes place. The relationship is confidential. The mentee should do lot of the leg work. Mentoring promotes transformational leadership.

Eric Parsloe of the Oxford School of Coaching and Mentoring defines mentoring as "To support and encourage people to manage their own learning in order that they may maximize their potential, develop their skills, improve their performance, and become the person they want to be".

The origin of mentor can be ascribed to Greek mythology where Mentor was the close friend of Odysseus as well as the teacher for Telemakos who was the son of Odysseus. When Odysseus went on tour he handed over the responsibility of his son, Telemakos to his friend Mentor who took the guardianship. Mentor not only guarded the friend's son but also guided, advised and counseled until Odysseus returned. (Author's blog: <http://profmsr.blogspot.com>)

Examine several cases where it was applied in the past. Greek philosopher, Socrates mentored Plato. Plato mentored Aristotle and the latter in turn mentored Alexander.

Merits

Mentoring is catching across the world. It helps new employees to get grooved and groomed within the system. Besides, there are several advantages:

- Sets developmental goals.
- Uncorks the hidden potential.
- Brings synergy.
- Aligns with company's vision.
- Hones the leadership skills for the mentors.
- Helps in career advancement for the mentees.
- Plays a key role in knowledge management.
- Helps in increased productivity and financial performance.
- Helps in improving bottom line of the business.

Characteristics of Mentors

The primary role of mentors is to encourage and motivate their mentees or protégés. They should provide inspiration and direction. They should be accessible and approachable. They must be able to stand out from the crowd. The mentees must accept them like their role models. Mentors should be excellent listeners and must be in a position to maintain confidentiality about their mentees. They should have both sympathy and empathy towards their mentees.

Mentors should enhance the self-confidence of mentee. They must be persons of principles. They must be specialized in their field. They must have attained good education, experience and expertise in their domains. In brief, mentor should be like a guide, facilitator, philosopher, counselor, psychologist, teacher, trainer, leader, adviser and motivator.

Merits for Mentor

Mentoring has merits for both mentors and mentees. When observed from the perspective of mentor, there are several advantages. It helps in sharing the knowledge, experience, competencies that have been acquired over many years. There is an element of great satisfaction when sharing success, expertise and experience with others. It offers wider scope for experimentation and visibility.

Mentoring takes the mentor to the next higher level thus fulfilling self-actualization needs. There is huge potential to generate new vibes. It enables more self-confidence, self-esteem and self-satisfaction. Leaving a legacy through your mentee and becoming a legend gives you immense pleasure. The mentor becomes the reservoir of more knowledge as the saying goes "Knowledge grows when shared". It develops coaching and leadership skills. It is indeed an enriching experience to become a mentor.

Characteristics for Mentee

Mentee must have lot of patience and perseverance. Passion to learn and grow should be the hallmark. It is essential to regard and respect mentor. Mentee should be proactive and initiator. Mentee should have ability to experiment and go extra mile. She/he should persevere whenever the mentor is busy. And s/he should be prepared mentally for leg work. Taking feedback is necessary for improvement. S/he must come out of his/her comfort zone and enter into effective zone. And s/he must be able to accept criticism gracefully without any false ego.

Merits for Mentee

"The ripest peach is highest on the tree."

- Helps in discovering hidden potential.
- Helps in learning the ropes.
- Equips with skills, abilities and competencies thus enhancing career advancement.
- Enhances effectiveness rather efficiency.
- Avoids any kind of dissatisfaction with work.
- Bridges the gap between expectations and realities.
- Acquires specialized expertise.
- Develops networking abilities.

- Builds self-confidence.
- Widens career opportunities.

Mentoring Benefits to Organizations

Companies are realizing the importance of mentor training for their employees. The benefits are plenty. Mentoring enhances the productivity and performance of the employees. It ultimately strengthens the companies' bottom line. It minimizes the misunderstandings among the employees thus enhancing effective communication and interpersonal skills. Mentoring brings the people closer in companies. It improves team building skills and enhances knowledge base. Overall it improves soft skills among the employees thus ensuring organizational growth and prosperity.

Types of Mentoring

There are various types of mentoring. A few of them in brief are: Informal or natural mentoring, developmental mentoring, peer mentoring, student mentoring, youth mentoring, team mentoring, business mentoring, political mentoring, lateral mentoring, soft (skills) mentoring, facilitated mentoring, reverse mentoring, entrepreneurial mentoring etc., It is an evolving and emerging area where new concepts surface regularly.

Mentoring Stages

Zachary (2000), in her book The Mentor's Guide, describes the mentoring process in four stages. These are preparing, negotiating, enabling, and coming to closure.

During the preparing stage, the mentee prepares the ground for meeting the mentor who suits his/her goals. Mentee searches for several mentors through various ways and means and finally selects the mentor. Mentee looks at the competency of the mentor, matching his/her goal requirements, time availability, accessibility, affordability and convenience.

It is rightly said, "If a drop of water falls in a lake there is no identity. But if it falls on a leaf of lotus it shines like a pearl. So choose the best place where you can shine". Therefore, choosing the right mentor is the first step towards successful mentoring.

Once s/he selects the right mentor then s/he approaches the mentor for services. S/he negotiates and creates a common ground for launching. If both mentor and mentee feel comfortable with the domain and other parameters and formalities then they proceed to the third stage of mentoring process.

Enabling is the most critical and crucial stage where the real mentoring takes place. There may be practical problems and bottlenecks that have to be sorted out for smooth execution of enabling. There could be differences of opinions and perceptions. Efforts are to be made to bridge the gap, if any. However, it is always easier said than done.

After the successful completion of this stage, the final stage of closure comes where in both relationship between mentor and mentee comes to an end. The entire process can be compared with that of a research guide and research scholar for doing PhD work.

Yet another four stages of mentoring relationship outlined by Linda Watt are: Initiation, Cultivation, Separation and Re-definition. (By Linda Watt for ACERRA)

It is essential to conduct SWOT (Strengths, Weaknesses, Opportunities and Threats) analysis for both mentor and mentee to check whether chemistry and synergy exists between the interests of both. Thorough analysis also helps to leverage benefits. Besides, it eliminates, any fiasco during the process.

During mentoring, all efforts should be made to make mentee independent. The feedback about the process has to be objective and specific. It should not be aimed at personal criticism but at the behavior for bringing necessary improvements. Mentoring should not deviate from the desired goals. It should be focused clearly.

During the process of mentoring the mentor must encourage the mentee by calling *'You can do it', 'I believe in you', 'I like your mesmerizing speech', 'You are progressing well', 'You are unique', 'I am learning certain things from you', 'As a mentor I have discovered my own strengths', 'Your smile is magical', 'Do you need any assistance?'* etc. All these things are to be applied according to the strengths of each mentee and also depending on the cultural backgrounds. (Author's Blog: <http://profmsr.blogspot.com>)

Mentoring is not a spoon feeding. It is a type of fine-tuning the mentee. Mentor is not expected to answer all queries of the mentee. Mentor is not a dumping ground to put in everything. The mentor and the process of mentoring have to be respected. The relation goes on mutual trust and respect. Mentoring is not an affair but marriage like scenario where permanent relations are involved.

Myths and Truths about Mentoring

The first myth is that age of mentor should be more than mentee. It is a mistaken belief. The truth is that it is the experience and expertise in the professional front, not the age that counts. At times, the domain expertise makes a younger person to mentor the older person.

The second myth is that the relationship benefits only either mentor or mentee. On the other hand, mentoring is beneficial for both mentor and mentee. The truth is that the mentor also learns while teaching and the mentee learns from the experiences of the mentor.

The third myth is that once the mentoring is over, the relationship ends between both. Although the formal relation ends once the mentoring process is completed, the truth is that it may lead to long lasting relations between the both.

Blending Inside and Outside Mentors

For effective leadership mentoring, it is necessary to have both inside mentors and outside mentors.

The inside mentors are those mentors who are domain experts and seniors with in the organization. Where as, the outside mentors are the domain experts without any organizational affinity. The inside mentors are very much aware of the organizational problems practically as they have been working within the system for some time. If the mentors feel that the mentee has more capability than the mentor other than the organizational expertise, they may develop a kind of insecurity resulting into jealousy and organizational politics. There is also a possibility of not revealing the trade secrets about the organization and the practical problems involved to the mentee. The inside mentors may not reveal the smart work they adopt while execution of tasks with apprehensions of mentee outsmarting or overtaking them. Above all, ego problems may crop up during mentoring thus complicating and worsening the mentoring process.

In the case of outside mentors, they do not have to think of organizational politics as they are outside the organization. They just believe in providing basic inputs, competencies, skills of the domain to make the mentee capable of delivering the goods. These people do not have to worry about their mentee superseding or surpassing them as they will not work with them.

In a nutshell, the inside mentors stress on hard work and the outside mentors on smart work. The inside mentors highlight in practices and outside mentors emphasizes in theory. The former focuses on survival and the latter on success. Inside mentoring teaches about soft skills and outside mentoring teaches about hard skills. Therefore, it is essential to focus on blending both inside and outside mentors for attaining organizational effectiveness.

Takeaways

What we have done for ourselves alone dies with us. What we have done for others and the world remains and is immortal.- Albert Pine

Mentoring is not new. Right from stone age to space age and from Industrial age to Information age mentoring has been existing. It will exist as long as the human civilization exists.

Having mentor is essential. You lose nothing but gain a lot. It is cost-effective and in few cases no money is involved. Mentoring offers risk free returns. Every individual owes something towards society. Keeping knowledge within themselves does not bring any results to the mankind. All individuals must learn to give their best for the benefit of mankind. Let us leave the world better than what we found.

KEY TERMS

- Killer instinct
- Humility
- Common skills
- Hard skills
- Communication skills
- Assertiveness
- Team building
- Networking skills
- Soft skills
- NLP
- Body language
- Mentoring

BRAINSTORMING EXERCISES

- Did you display killer instinct at any point of time? When? Explain the thrill of it and endeavour to apply again.
- As a leader how can you build a team? Explain the process and challenges involved in team building.
- Explain humility and illustrate a few people you have come across in your life.
- Are networking skills essential to come up in life? Explain with your real life experiences where you utilized network for achieving your goals.
- Mention the common skills which are required to everyone and justify.
- Illustrate common, soft and hard skills with examples.
- State how does NLP promote your communication skills?
- How to do improve your body language?

ACTIVITIES

Make a group of friends and enact the body language postures mentioned in this chapter and take feedback from others. Practice thoroughly. It improves your body language and your performance in socializing with others.

Record your conversation with others in a video for 30 minutes. Play the same by muting the oral communication and check for the movement of your body postures. You will get to know more about your body language.

REFERENCES

Author's Blog: <http://profmsr.blogspot.com/>

<http://www.gp-training.net/training/communication_skills/nlp/quotes_nlp.htm>

<http://www.ppimk.com/NLP/NLP-What.html>

<http://www.thecoachinginstitute.com.au/what-is-nlp.html>

Zachary, L. J. (2000). The mentor's guide: Facilitating effective learning relationships. San Francisco: Jossey Bass,

Zachary, L. J. What leaders must do to ensure mentoring success,

Eric Parsloe of the Oxford School of Coaching and Mentoring, by Linda Watt for ACERRA,

'A Life That Counts' by Dr.John C. Maxwell.

5

TOOLS FOR YOUR SUCCESS

If you want to be truly successful, invest in yourself to get the knowledge you need to find your unique factor. When you find it and focus on it and persevere, your success will blossom. — Sydney Madwed

LEARNING OBJECTIVES

After reading this chapter and doing the exercises, you should be able to:

- Know how to brand yourself.
- Take care of your health for achieving success.
- Appreciate the importance of money and generate multiple sources of income.
- Assess your behavioural style.
- Judge your personality through MBTI.
- Describe the process of decision making.
- Manage your mind effectively.
- Enhance your memory.
- Realise the significance of solitude.
- Differentiate between motivation and inspiration.
- Learn lessons out of failures.
- Overcome depression.
- Manage your anger.
- Balance your work and life successfully.
- Understand types of feedback and know the knack of giving and taking feedback.

CHAPTER OUTLINE

1. Personal branding
2. Health is wealth

3. Financial freedom is fortitude
4. Four behavioural styles
5. MBTI
6. Decision making
7. Mind management
8. Memory techniques
9. Solitude is fortitude
10. Motivation and inspiration
11. Facing failures
12. How to overcome depression?
13. Managing your anger
14. How to maintain work-life balance?
15. How to give feedback?

PERSONAL BRANDING

We are judged by what we finish, not what we start. - Anonymous

Personal branding has become the order of the day for recalling and achieving success. It helps you to stand separately from the crowd. You need to be different from others in terms of talents, abilities and skills. It is essential to go by the road that is less traveled.

While branding yourself, you have to look at your inherent talents and build your portfolio. Besides, look at your skills and abilities that can support and sustain you toward success. When you combine your truck load of talents with your passionate skills and abilities branding yourself becomes easier task. When you look at famous cricketers like Sachin, Ganguly and Dhoni people recall each cricketer with a specialization although all these three are cricketers. Branding helps in memory recall. Develop your niche areas and project yourself regularly and over a period of time people call you as so and so. Once you are branded, you should not be complacent. Keep reinventing yourself by adopting changes regularly. We can take leaves out of various celebrities like Amitabh, Amir Khan, Shahrukh Khan, Vijay Mallya, etc., in personal branding.

HEALTH IS WEALTH

It is health that is real wealth and not pieces of gold and silver. - Mahatma Gandhi

People often give so much of importance to materialistic considerations rather than to health. They earn a lot but unfortunately they shell out a lot to medical expenses. Besides, they don't enjoy blissful life due to health complications despite being wealthy. They are subject to fatigue and mental tension. When people focus too much on materialistic and worldly pleasures they tend to neglect their health. As a result, they suffer at the end. For instance, the pop star, Michael Jackson had lot of wealth but unfortunately his poor health cost his life. A few celebrities suffer with several health complications despite being blessed with lot of wealth. In this context, given below are a few tips for maintaining good health.

Tips for Good Health

The first wealth is health. - Ralph Waldo Emerson

- Hit gym regularly. A regular exercise enhances life expectancy and longevity and keeps agile and active.
- Involve in physical activities wherever it is possible. Prefer to climb stairs rather than to escalators or elevators.
- Avoid alcoholism. Excessive drinking is always unhealthy.
- If you lead a sedentary lifestyle then it is time you need to exercise your body. Those who work with computer systems should take break at regular intervals of time and walk around for lifting their energy levels.
- Go for swimming regularly as entire body gets worked out during swimming resulting into overall physical fitness.
- Drink lot of water as it energizes body and hydrates the system.
- Always take nutritious food especially fruits and salads. Avoid junk food, oily and fatty food.
- Consume a diet that is rich in carbohydrates just before and after a heavy work out for better health.
- Take food at regular intervals of time for better digestion.
- Go either for yoga or meditation.
- Go to a serene place and spend time as solitude is fortitude.
- Say no to drugs and tobacco.
- Go to bed at regular time everyday.
- Go for regular medical check up.
- Never brood over the unpleasant past as it not only disturbs peace of mind but also wastes time.
- Go for a stroll with family members once in a while as it promotes better understanding among the family members and relaxes your mind.

Takeaways

He who has health has hope, and he who has hope has everything. -Arabian Proverb

Although technology has brought several comforts to mankind it has also brought out complexities. Life has become highly challenging with lot of uncertainty and complexity. People should realize the importance of health and spend some time daily on health oriented activities. Spending time on regular fitness should not be treated as an expense rather an investment. You can achieve anything and everything if health is good. To sum up, health is more important than wealth.

FINANCIAL FREEDOM IS FORTITUDE

Freedom is not merely the opportunity to do as one pleases; neither is it merely the opportunity to choose between set alternatives. Freedom is, first of all, the chance to formulate the available choices, to argue over them — and then, the opportunity to choose. - C. Wright Mills

The 21st century has thrown several challenges to mankind. Apart from creating lot of uncertainty and complexity with the drastic changes in rapid growing technology, it also made people to think deeply about financial freedom. Man cannot survive without money. Money has become almost a necessary evil. In the name of acquiring money, people struggle a lot and a few make mistakes to earn money for their survival and few make mistakes to amass wealth. People are made to think that money is success.

Money will not buy happiness but it provides a sense of security. Money is only a means not an end. Unfortunately, for many people, money has become an end resulting into unethical practices. In this context, let us know what is all about financial freedom.

What is Financial Freedom?

Lack of money is the root of all evil. - George Bernard Shaw

What do you mean by financial freedom? Is it having sufficient money to live off forever without working? Is it having income more than expense? Is it being debt free? Is it the freedom to do anything and everything with money? It is very difficult to define financial freedom as there is no yardstick to measure. It is, in fact, a complex one. Financial freedom differs from person to person.

Financial freedom is more about your attitude towards money rather than about the amount of money you have. It is also about having sufficient money to lead your life comfortably without any botheration. It is not being too much rich but being comfortable with sufficient financial reserves to back you up in case of any eventuality. It is like having money beyond your break even point *i.e.,* the point where your income flow is higher than expenses.

There are two types of incomes such as active and passive income. In active income, the individual is actively involved in generating income. On the other hand, in passive income the money flows without active involvement of the individual. The rental income, returns on share market investments, income as a sleeping partner in business and royalties out of publications fall in the category of passive income.

Tips for Financial Freedom

Money isn't everything—but it's a long way ahead of what comes next. - Edmund Stockdale

- Sit in a quiet place and ponder ways towards financial freedom.
- Develop a positive attitude towards money.
- Minimize spending and maximize savings.
- Generate multiple sources of income.
- Don't save until you clear your debts, if any.
- Go for cost cutting whe1ever it is possible.
- Buy in cash not on credit as the cost of the goods will go up on credit purchases thereby denting your reserves.
- Be good at accounting and budgeting. Many people fail miserably in these two areas resulting into financial chaos.
- Work hard and work smart as well. You need to make sure that your money should make money. Your money should rotate.

- Set SMART financial goals where S stands for specific, M for measurable, A for achievable, R for reachable and T for time-bound.
- Diversify the risk. Don't keep all eggs in one basket. Invest little in savings, share market, gold, land and other areas. In case of crisis in one area, the other areas can back you up.
- Work from home, if possible. Now -a-days, there are so many opportunities to generate incomes through home based businesses.
- Convert your passion into profession and make your passion as a business opportunity.

Takeaways

Earn all you can, save all you can, give all you can. - Charles Wesley

Only when you have financial freedom you will be able to concentrate on other creative pursuits. Have the mindset of a rich person. It is all there in your mind. If you have mindset and urge to make money you can definitely make money. Penny saved is penny earned. Cultivate savings attitude. Save for the rainy day as life is full of uncertainty and complexity.

Financial freedom is all about your attitude towards money and your aptitude to make money. Wipe out the old notion of *'making money is a sin'*. Parents need to cultivate right attitude about financial freedom among their children in the initial stage itself as they learn to save, manage and enjoy money. It helps them to know the value of money and how it plays a crucial role in having comforts and facilities and leading a successful and peaceful life. To conclude, financial freedom is, indeed, fortitude.

FOUR BEHAVIOURAL STYLES

We observe various kinds of behaviors when we interact with people. An individual's behavior basically depends on his heredity background, socialization, perceptions and attitude. Briefly behavior can be classified into four styles. They are Expressive style, Amiable style, Analytical style and Driver style.

Individuals belong to Amiable style are usually quiet and others can work with them at ease and comfort as they are cooperative. They are flexible and adaptable. They tend to avoid risk and like to play safe in their endeavors. They are loyal to the individuals and institutions and work with dedication and discipline. They are good listeners, empathize with others and can work in teams without any ego clashes and conflicts.

However, the individuals belong to Analytical style are practical oriented and have eye for detail and follow procedures strictly. Risk avoidance is the quality of this style. Before taking any decision, they consult experts and weigh all options and then resort to decision making. They are thorough professionals and businesslike and looks for permutations and combinations before taking a final call. They are highly disciplined and like to be independent. They strongly believe in relationships but at the same time they display little emotion when dealing with others.

The individuals in the Expressive style are emotional, outgoing and like to take initiative in their endeavors. They know how to inspire others and are aggressive in their behavior. They are highly energetic and ambitious. They are extrovert in nature and like to share their dreams and ideas. They crave for recognition and rewards. They are excellent in communication and networking skills.

In the case of individuals who belong to Driver style, they are very pushy, iron willed and strong headed. They are intuitive, believe in gut feeling and do not hesitate to go for conflicts. They do not let the things happen rather they make things happen. They speak to the point precisely and like to take the charge. Often entrepreneurs belong to this style. They are high risk takers and even if they fail and fall, they rise like phoenix.

To sum it up, we cannot say that a particular style is better than the other. Every style has niceties and pitfalls and every style is unique. Knowing various behavior styles help in promoting harmonious relations and will pave the way for your success.

MBTI (MYERS-BRIGGS TYPE INDICATOR)

Everyone thinks of changing the world, but no one thinks of changing himself. - Leo Tolstoy

The origin of the Myers-Briggs Type Indicator (MBTI) assessment goes to Carl Gustav Jung who laid foundation for this and the same was further developed by Katharine Cook Briggs and her daughter, Isabel Briggs Myers during the World War II. It was developed for the women entering the industrial workforce. The intention was to ensure that the women felt comfortable to work during war time jobs.

What is MBTI?

The MBTI is a psychometric instrument helps in finding out how people perceive the world and others in taking decisions. This psychometric instrument lists out the psychological differences into four dichotomies (Extraversion Introversion, Sensing iNtuition, Thinking Feeling, Judging Perceiving) which results into 16 possible psychological types. For instance, all these 16 types are listed out like ISTJ, ISFJ, INFJ, INTJ, ISTP, ISFP, INFP, INTP, ESTP, ESFP, ENFP, ENTP, ESTJ, ESFJ, ENFJ and ENTJ. It reveals from these tests that there is nothing right or wrong with the people's preferences.

It is believed that the people who are sensing look within five senses. In contrast, the people who are intuitive look beyond five senses for patterns and meaning. In a nutshell, sensors are present focused while the intuitors are future focused by nature.

Leadership Material

We judge ourselves by what we feel capable of doing, while others judge us by what we have already done. - Henry Wadsworth Longfellow

The research reveals that people with Thinking and Judging —TJ possess leadership material. It is because leaders need to possess the qualities of deep thinking and judging the people to carry them forward. Therefore, the people who possess TJ in their categories are sure to succeed as leaders. There are several advantages of taking MBTI test which are stated below.

Merits

It is the greatest good for an individual to discuss virtue (aka arete) every day...for the unexamined life is not worth living. - Socrates

- MBTI is widely used in corporate training for leadership development, team building skills, coaching, mentoring and marketing.

- It is very much useful for youth especially in the area of career counseling so that they can choose the right career and succeed professionally.
- It enhances the chances for students to succeed in interviews as well.
- It helps working professionals to face the challenges as they get to know about themselves thoroughly.
- It helps in getting into the right education based on aptitude thus enhancing the learning curve.
- It helps in SWOT (Strengths, Weaknesses, Opportunities and Threats) analysis and for problem solving.

Takeaways

Only by much searching and mining are gold and diamonds obtained, and man can find every truth connected with his being if he will dig deep into the mine of his soul. - James Allen

MBTI is useful to all be it for students, teachers, entrepreneurs, professionals etc., It helps in categorizing and classifying what group individuals belong. Therefore, they can make use of this test for their personal and professional growth. There are several online tests. Therefore, it is advisable to take the test and rate themselves. Besides, there is extra information about the global celebrities and personalities who belong to each category. MBTI helps in taking inspiration from such successful personalities.

DECISION-MAKING

Decision making is the specific executive task. - Peter F. Drucker

We all make decisions in life. But making an effective decision is indeed a tough task in today's borderless world. The challenge with decision making is that you won't always have all the data you need. However you need to make decision within the given constraints. Given below are the stages of decision-making that help in arriving at the right decisions.

Before arriving at the decision, it is necessary to establish a positive, healthy and conducive environment. It helps in free flow of ideas, opinions among the participating members. The leader of the team should not bias the members with his/her opinions and options as it stifles the decision-making process. Once the stage has been set the members must be allowed to provide divergent shades of opinions through several techniques like brainstorming, Delphi, mind mapping, reverse brainstorming etc., Evaluate the multiple alternatives by weighing the pros and cons through discussion and deliberation and followed by taking a call. Once the decision has been made it is time to check the viability and feasibility of the decision. Communicate the same to the team members and execute the decision. Finally it is time to check the validity and reliability through feedback

The above decision-making process helps in generating qualitative solutions for several problems.

MIND MANAGEMENT

You are the most powerful magnet in the universe! You contain a magnetic power within you that is more powerful than anything in this world, and this unfathomable magnetic power is emitted through your thoughts. - Rhonda Byrne

The human mind is an enigma. It is very powerful and has vast potential. However, people don't realize. They look elsewhere without realizing their hidden potential laying within them. Even if few people realize they don't know how to use their potential up to the hilt. In fact, those who win this world are the ones who know how to spot their hidden potential and realize the same for achieving success.

What is Mind Management?

The state of your life is nothing more than a reflection of your state of mind. — Wayne W. Dyer

Mind management is all about managing the mind effectively and efficiently. It is the process of exploring, analyzing, realizing, planning, organizing, directing, controlling and exploiting human mind for achieving all-round success in personal, professional and social life. It is related to self-awareness, self-introspection and self-development.

Through mind management you can achieve success. First of all, you must know all about mind management. Secondly, there is a methodology to tap and manage your hidden potential. Thirdly, by orienting your potential through right tools and techniques, you can connect to your outside world. And fourthly, by putting sustained efforts and energies regularly, you can achieve success.

Everything is there in your mind. It all depends on your state of thinking and management. Whether you want to have a triumph or a waterloo, it is in your hands. You need to build a right mental attitude through mind management which takes you towards success in your chosen area of interest.

Mind Management Process

Formulate and stamp indelibly on your mind a mental picture of yourself as succeeding. Hold this picture tenaciously. Never permit it to fade. Your mind will seek to develop the picture. - Norman Vincent Peale

As people maintain their physical body by hitting gym, or walking or exercising, they should maintain their mind qualitatively through right process.

Engage your mind everyday with certain targets. Early morning when you wake up from bed, write down what is to be executed so that your mind gets engaged throughout the day about the tasks.

Prepare the list of qualities to be developed. Find out the ways and means to develop the same. Jot down the resources required to reach and get equipped. Build bridges and network with relevant people. Don't invent excuses. Have firm will power and commitment to see through the things.

We run internal movies within our minds through self-talk. It is a narrator helps in shaping our minds. Whatever the positive or negative actions reflected in our lives is the result of self-talk running in our minds. In fact, you are the director of your mind.

You need to control your emotions, intellect and habits so as to develop right mental attitude. It helps in better mind management.

Everyday when you go to bed, take feedback about the progress of what was done and what has to be done the very next day. When you do so, your mind starts working in a focused manner.

Mind management is not possible in overnight. It requires lot of practice to develop a positive mindset. It must become an ingrained habit.

Tips

Your mind is an instrument, a tool. It is there to be used for a specific task, and when the task is completed, you lay it down. As it is, I would say about 80 to 90 percent of most people's thinking is not only repetitive and useless, but because of its dysfunctional and often negative nature, much of it is also harmful. Observe your mind and you will find this to be true. It causes a serious leakage of vital energy. - Eckhart Tolle

- Journal whatever pops up in your mind and prioritize. It helps in staying focused and also manages your time.
- Clear your mental clutter. Don't let negativity creep in your mind. As you sweep your house, you must clean your mind regularly by removing negative thoughts.
- Read good books that will uplift and inspire you.
- Listen to motivational audio tapes everyday.
- Write and visualize affirmations.
- Never criticize, condemn and complain as it keeps your mind free and healthy keeping more space for absorbing positive information.
- Be creative and pursue your passionate areas to keep your mind receptive and flexible.
- Avoid invalidating people who poison your mind with discouraging and negative comments. They also squash your dreams and limit your thinking.
- Avoid obsessive thinking as it clutters your mind.
- Avoid wet blankets.
- Have only realistic and achievable expectations.
- Have passion for continuous learning and growing.
- Learn to forgive and forget.
- Observe solitude as it reinvigorates and revives your mental powers. In fact, solitude is fortitude.

Takeaways

What we think determines what happens to us, so if we want to change our lives, we need to stretch our minds. - Wayne Dyer

Success should start from you and from within yourself. For this, you need to manage your mind. You need to orient your mind towards goals. Once it is done, you need to put in sustained efforts and energies to achieve. If you want to win a battle you need to win it in your mind first and then in real life. Similarly, if you want to achieve success you need to achieve it in your mind so that you can translate into reality.

You can grow your mind the way you grow your body physically. How you nurture your mind is in your hands. What kind of inputs and instructions you give is in your hands. Your results will depend on your efforts. To put it succinctly, your efforts are directly proportional to your results.

Your future is in your hands. Take the right step. Give something back to this world and bring difference in the lives of others.

MEMORY TECHNIQUES

Some memories are realities, and are better than anything that can ever happen to one again. - Willa Cather

People often confuse between weak memory and poor recollection. They complain of weak memory. In fact, it is not weak memory but poor collection of information. How sad it is when you cannot recall the name of a person you met in the past. What impression does it convey to other person when you regrettably say that you forgot his name?

In this busy and competitive world people forget the telephone numbers, passwords and pin numbers. It not only stops the work but also causes irritation for not remembering. Sometimes, you curse yourself for not remembering the things. There are several tools and techniques by which you can improve your memory. It is not a big challenge but it requires little more concentration and effort. Human brain is highly complex. You must know how to make use of it to improve your memory. In this context, it is desirable to know briefly about memory.

What is Memory?

Memory is the diary that we all carry about with us. - Oscar Wilde.

Memory is a mental activity where in stored information is recalled and retrieved as and when required. It is divided into two types: short-term and long-term. In short-term memory, the information is stored for a few seconds or minutes. In contrast, in long-term memory, the information is stored for longer duration. When people listen to others, they feed in their memory automatically whether to register for short-term or long-term depending on the importance of information.

Memory Tips

All improvement in memory consists of one's habitual method of recording facts. - Dr. William James.

- Open up your mind and instruct to encode new information.
- Concentration is the key to good memory. Explore ways to enhance your concentration.
- Stay focused on one thing at a time. Don't go for multitasking. Whenever you feel that the information is important you need to put in more efforts and concentration so that you can remember well.
- Avoid noises, interruptions and external disturbances while listening.
- Do things slowly as it reinforces your memory.
- Call people by names when introduced. For instance, "It is my pleasure to meet you, Robert". Associate name of the people with well known people you have already registered in your mind for better retention. Create visual pictures in your mind.
- When you speak louder you can remember better as you listen to your own voice. Maintain diary to jot down the important information.
- Prioritize the information while receiving. It helps in retaining the important information. Instead of typing the information, you may write with your hand as the muscular memory will be activated resulting into storing the information.

- There are several games on television and online to enhance your memory. Playing the same will prove to be helpful.
- Assimilate the information rather than reading the content for the sake of reading. It aids your memory.
- If you find it difficult to memorize large content, you can break it into small parts. Memorize each small part and mentally compile the same for final memorization.
- Relate the information with your real live events through pictorial visualization as it helps in recollection.
- Research reveals that humans can remember between 5 to 9 items at a time. If you can break the information between 5 to 9 items then it becomes easy for you to remember and recollect.
- People have natural tendency to remember rhymes and rhythms. Therefore, convert your content accordingly for effective memory.
- Go to bed without overly worried about anything. If you go to bed thinking about the problems then you get better solutions by the next day morning.
- Relax your mind when blocked with memory recall. Engage your mind on other issues. To your surprise you will recall whatever you wanted as your brain searches for the information.
- Avoid anxiety and stress as it blocks your memory. Adopt relaxation techniques.
- Make use of your inner dialogue. Every individual involves in self-talk which is also known as inner dialogue. Repeated conversation within your mind reinforces and aids your memory.
- When you talk new concepts with others, it not only improves your communication skills but also aids in memorizing complicated information.
- The way you exercise your body you should exercise your memory muscles.
- Finally, take nutritious food as it keeps your body and mind healthy. It aids in effective memory.

Memory Techniques for Students

The true art of memory is the art of attention. - Samuel Johnson.

1. Students should review the information they receive in the classroom within a day so that they can retain the same effectively. Jotting down the points taught during the class by teacher helps them to review and revise immediately.
2. Students should focus on the key words while reading the content as it helps them in analyzing, understanding and memorizing the content. Read the content repeatedly if possible.
3. Develop your own mnemonic device where in the first letters of each word have to be framed as a word for better recalling. It helps students especially during examinations.
4. Use highlighters and colored pens while reading the text and apply the same depending on the importance and priority of the content. It helps in saving time and also in better memory.
5. Find out what kind of senses would be comfortable and ideal for you and exploit the same for better memory.

6. "A picture is worth thousand words" goes the saying. Use pictures, graphs and charts to help your memory.
7. Write and rewrite the content repeatedly as it enriches your content apart from aiding your memory.

Takeaways

Memory is the mother of all wisdom. - Aeschylus.

Memory is not the privilege of a gifted few. If you know that it is a skill you can cultivate easily. But you need to put in efforts regularly for achieving amazing results. Memory tips help everyone including children, students and working people for achieving success. We all are blessed with good memory. Unfortunately, we don't realize and exploit. Effective utilization of memory helps in better interpersonal relations, builds bridges and ensures all round success.

SOLITUDE IS FORTITUDE

We live in a very tense society. We are pulled apart... and we all need to learn how to pull ourselves together.... I think that at least part of the answer lies in solitude. - Helen Hayes

Life is becoming more complex with the rapid changing technology. Stress levels among the people are rising at alarming rates with the rising aspirations and expectations of the people. Companies demand a lot from their employees to beat the stiff competition which is possible only by being innovative and creative in delivery of goods and services. In this process, employees undergo fatigue at the workplace resulting into higher stress levels. Employees also want to prove and survive themselves by going extra mile. It is in this context, solitude is the need of the hour to break stress, anxiety monotony and boredom.

What is Solitude?

Inside myself is a place where I live all alone, and that's where I renew my springs that never dry up. - Pearl Buck

People often confuse between solitude with loneliness. In fact, it is not so. Solitude is a state of being alone for a short-term where in there will not be any physical contact with others. It is like taking a break once in a week by totally avoiding the routine work. It is also like taking a short leave for vacation. As people go for fasting without taking food for giving rest to the internal system, people also go for solitude for giving rest to mind for sometime.

Loneliness vs Solitude

We enter the world alone, we leave it alone. - James Anthony Froude

Often loneliness and solitude are interchangeably used by people. However, there is a thin line separating these both. Loneliness is a negative state whereas solitude is a positive state. Solitude helps in engaging oneself internally with a healthy thought process as a companion. Loneliness reflects missing something in life. It represents isolation. Loneliness depletes mind and body while solitude restores. Loneliness is bitterness while solitude is sweetness. To put it succinctly, solitude is chosen while loneliness is imposed.

Merits

True silence is the rest of the mind, and is to the spirit what sleep is to the body, nourishment and refreshment. - William Penn

- It is the best way to get to know about yourself.
- It removes the clutter and purifies your mind thus enhancing your concentration.
- It helps in beating stress levels.
- It helps you dig deep within and brings out the best.
- It helps in better self-awareness, self-control and self-discipline.
- It helps in recouping the lost energies. Besides, it builds fresh energies, enhances creativity and innovation.
- It helps in exploring yourself analytically thus improving your personality for all-round success.
- It replenishes your energies and helps you move further and forward with confidence and optimism.

Solitude is Fortitude

No man should go through life without once experiencing healthy, even bored solitude in the wilderness, finding himself depending solely on himself and thereby learning his true and hidden strength. - Jack Kerouac

When you do routine things you get bored. Then, it is time to go for solitude for self-analysis and introspection. When you want to do things differently, it is time to go for solitude. People go to beaches and spend time in solitude in the sounds of sea waves as it provides solace and strengthens will-power.

History reveals that several great leaders preferred solitude whenever they were in distress. In the epic Mahabharat, at the fag end of Kurukshetra battle, Duryodana underwent inside the water to remain calm for sometime and also to take in fresh energies. It was a kind of solitude. Saints and sages go for solitude to search themselves internally. They go to a serene place and enjoy in a state of solitariness. Therefore, solitude is fortitude.

Takeaways

Solitude shows us what should be; society shows us what we are. - Robert Cecil

People should spend sometime in solitude everyday so as to stay healthy physically, mentally and spiritually. It should be treated as an investment and expense of time. Few companies provide sabbatical leave to their employees who work for some period. It helps them to unwind themselves and get back to work with recharged energies. To sum up, it is essential for individuals and institutions to go for solitude regularly keeping in view of the growing uncertainty and complexity due to rapid technology.

The happiest of all lives is a busy solitude. - Voltaire

MOTIVATION AND INSPIRATION

Man's greatest glory is not in never failing, but in rising up every time he falls. — Oliver Goldsmith.

He failed in business at 21 years. He was defeated in elections at 22 years. Again he failed in business at 24 years. He lost his wife at 26 years and had nervous breakdown at 27 years. He lost senatorial elections at 45 years, lost elections as Vice-President at 47 and again at 49 years. Ultimately he became the President of America at 52 years. By this time, it is obvious to every reader that he was none other than Abraham Lincoln. What do we call his spirit? Can we call it as motivation? Certainly, Yes. Success is product of successive setbacks. The word motivation is coined from the Latin word "movere", which means to move. Motivation can be defined as an internal drive that activates behavior and gives it direction. To put it succinctly, the ability to move from one failure to another without losing energy and enthusiasm is known as motivation. If someone achieves success after a success without any setbacks, can we call it as motivation? Of course, Not. By the way, let us know the definition of motivation from Wikipedia also.

Motivation (Wikipedia) is the reason or reasons for engaging in a particular behavior, especially human behavior as studied in psychology and neuropsychology. These reasons may include basic needs such as food or a desired object, hobbies, goal, state of being, or ideal. The motivation for a behavior may also be attributed to less-apparent reasons such as altruism or morality. According to Geen, [#] motivation refers to the initiation, direction, intensity and persistence of human behavior.

Motivation and Inspiration

Often people confuse between motivation and inspiration. Motivation comes out of external influence that encourages you either with ideas or with individuals. While in inspiration, it comes from with in and with internal influence. Inspiration results in a feeling of excitement and well being, and a desire to get into action instantly without any prompting while motivation needs prompting and encouragement by others.

Motivation comes from the word 'motivate' that means 'a stir to action'. On the other hand, inspiration comes from the word 'inspire' that means 'to fill with noble or reverent emotion'. In a nutshell, motivation stirs you while the inspiration fills you. And that is one of the major differences between the both. In many ways inspiration is bigger than motivation and, in fact, inspiration is more enduring and everlasting. You become inspired and you get motivated and that makes the subtle difference between the both. Many a time success is the product of both inspiration and motivation.

Merits

1. Motivation helps in shaping ones personality.
2. It helps individuals grow personally and professionally.
3. Helps in building positive and healthy circle of friends.
4. Helps in dreaming big and achieving big by removing negative thoughts.
5. Helps in achieving goals and objectives and makes life more meaningful.
6. Builds the bricks towards positive attitude.
7. Enhances self-confidence and self-esteem.
8. Makes an ordinary man as an extra-ordinary man.

Types

Basically there are three types of motivation such as internal motivation, external motivation and incentive motivation. In internal motivation, the individuals get motivated by themselves by various ways and means without expecting any external support. In this scenario the individuals have extraordinary will power and they constantly and continuously motivate themselves whenever faced with failures and then rise like Phoenix. It can also be called as self-motivation. It is the hallmark of great leaders. In the case of external motivation, the individuals are motivated by means of external influences by way of inspirational songs, slogans, pictures and persons. When the individuals are motivated due to monetary reasons, which usually happens in the corporate world, it is known as incentive or monetary motivation. Both internal and external motivation does not involve monetary aspects and hence belong to non-financial motivation.

Takeaways

Motivation is built on the bricks of optimism and confidence. These two fundamental factors are the driving forces towards higher motivational levels. It is necessary to get motivated all the times so as to succeed in personal, professional and social life. It is equally more important to motivate so as to motivate others. Problems are part of life and each problem will teach many lessons and makes an individual tough. When the going gets tough, the tough gets going. It is a well-admitted fact that a smooth sea never makes a skillful mariner. And success touches to the toes of skillful mariners only.

FACING FAILURES

Only those who dare to fail greatly can achieve greatly. - Robert F Kennedy

Facing failure and criticism is the most challenging task for any human being. Everyone loves success and hates failure. This is inherent in the human nature. Is it possible to achieve success without failure? Of course, it is not possible. By the way shall we define failure?

What is Failure?

It is always the gap between the expectations and the reality. When the outcome is against our predictions despite putting sincere efforts and energies then it is termed as failure. Outcome may be against us either due to internal factors like unknown mistakes or due to external forces which are beyond human control.

Importance of Failure

Failure brings down excessive ego and makes an individual humble and simple. It also eliminates overconfidence among the individuals. Failure helps in making the individual highly focused on goals and objectives. Some people feel too big for their shoes. Failure helps them to resize the same. It makes the people more tolerant and they start empathizing with others. Failure makes people flexible, receptive and more accommodative.

Tips after Facing Failure

- Keep cool and composed. Any extra activities at this juncture results into adding fuel to the fire. When faced with failure, human mind gets tense and does not think logically and analytically. Hence, do not become hasty.
- "Ninety nine per cent of all failures come from people who have a habit of making excuses" said George Washington Carver. Don't show your anger of your failure on others. When you are responsible for the failure then what is the meaning in transferring your anger on others?
- Go by bottom-up-approach by looking at the root of the problem and tackling it accordingly.
- If the root of the problem is big then slice it down into small pieces and analyze the individual slices independently and integrate the same.
- Immediately think how you went wrong and where you went wrong. Thorough analysis helps diagnose the reasons behind the failure and what transpired and prompted failure. This step will help in introspection and provides remedial action so that the mistakes are not repeated in future.
- Look clearly whether the failure is the result of internal factors or external forces which are beyond human control. If the mistake occurred due to external forces then it is futile to think through it. If the mistake occurred due to internal factors then this is the time to rectify and take remedial steps.
- Accept the fact that failure is universal. Let us know and accept the fact that small achievers have small failures and big achievers have big failure. It is a well admitted fact that higher the fall higher the rise. Think your failure is small when compared with others' as it brings solace to you.
- Take it up as a challenge. Don't take every problem as a problem; rather treat it as an opportunity. It is only the test of fire that makes a fine steel. An optimist looks for opportunities from problems where as pessimist looks for problems in each opportunity.
- Discuss the failure with your trusted colleagues and friends who can provide right direction and guidance. Discussion generates wider dimensions and helps to get at the broader format for failure.

Takeaways

Arrogance brings you down and humbleness brings you up. When you get tumble you get humble. Bounce back from failure like a rubber ball.

History has demonstrated that the most notable winners usually encountered heartbreaking obstacles before they triumphed. They won because they refused to become discouraged by their defeats. — B.C.Forbes.

HOW TO OVERCOME DEPRESSION?

Do not brood over your past mistakes and failures as this will only fill your mind with grief, regret and depression. Do not repeat them in the future. - Sivananda

Although technology has brought out several advantages to the mankind it has also brought out several disadvantages. One of the major demerits is depression. Depression was prevailing even in the ancient days. But it has become rampant now due to the growing complexities and uncertainty in the world.

What is Depression?

Depression is a state of mind where an individual is anxious due to several reasons. It is a state where an individual constantly broods about a problem which may be imaginary or real. It is a kind of sinking feeling and void. Depression is not mere sadness. It is beyond sadness. When people are let down by their loved ones they get depressed. When people don't reach their cherished goals and objectives, they get depressed.

In olden days, people used to approach religious leaders or gurus whenever they had the symptoms of depression. They used to ask several questions and diagnose the problem by boosting the confidence of the afflicted person.

Causes

There are several causes for getting into depression. Repeatedly thinking about the negative happenings of the past may lead to depression. We all make mistakes. There is nothing to recall repeatedly about the mistakes. Mistakes help us grow as refined individuals provided we learn lessons. Both genetic and biological factors are also responsible for depression. It may affect more among the weak willed persons.

Successive failures may result into depression thinking that there is something wrong with the approach. The problem lies in rectifying the approach rather than being unduly worried about the approach. At times, workplace conflicts may lead to depression. When people are not understood well by others they tend to get depressed. In such situations, talking to the people directly is the only solution. Lack of love and affection from near ones, feeling loneliness, early childhood abuse, financial problems, substance abuse, and alcoholism give rise to depressed state of mind.

When people do something guilty and when something is done against their wishes they may get into depression. The bad memories will haunt them forever. Usually neurotransmitters that occur in brain and hormonal imbalances are responsible to depression. When they are in deep water they will feel it. When they are in financial debt the depression starts.

When divorced people don't find right partners to share their feelings and sex, they may develop depression. When the sexual desires are not fulfilled due to lack of body chemistry between wife and husband, it may result into depression.

The challenge in the present world is that everybody wants to be a leader and nobody likes to a follower. People want success in overnight and in some cases they want success at any cost. When people set unrealistic goals they will not be able to achieve resulting into desperation. Likewise there are number of causes responsible for depression.

Effects

There is lot of negative fallout arising out of depression. When people are in depression entire world looks to be bad, the people around themselves appear to be bad and in fact they feel bad about themselves. The afflicted people may not get sound sleep which is known as insomnia (sleeplessness) or may sleep for longer time which is known as hypersomnia (oversleeping). People develop anxiety and unfounded fears and phobias and it may also lead to dysentery. It may also lead to lack of concentration and appetite, irritability and in few cases it may lead to suicidal tendencies.

How to Overcome?

Good humor is a tonic for mind and body. It is the best antidote for anxiety and depression. It is a business asset. It attracts and keeps friends. It lightens human burdens. It is the direct route to serenity and contentment. - Grenville Kleiser

Depression is like any other ailment and it can be cured. It is essential to find the underlying causes of depression. Once those are found, it is easy to address the problem through right medication and psychotherapy. Psychotherapy plays a crucial role in overcoming the depression. Psychotherapy is the process of treating the afflicted by involving in conversation. It helps in digging out what is bugging the afflicted and finding the appropriate solutions to the problem. Below are a few tips to overcome from depression.

- Everyone feels depression at some point of time. Don't succumb to depression. Fight back. Don't become hopeless and helpless.
- Seek professional help. Consult psychotherapists and experts who can counsel you.
- Always surround with positive and motivated individuals.
- Go for meditation or yoga.
- Never brood over issues but think over ideas.
- Listen to soft music or the music that touches and energies you.
- Break your thought process by switching to other creative and constructive areas and activities.
- Write down what is bugging you. It vents out our inner feelings.
- Always engage your mind in progressive and developmental activities.
- Never think that it is the end of life. Think that it is only towards betterment.
- Keep your mind in your control. Don't let depression control your mind.
- Share your feelings and emotions with others as it unburdens you. It will also give rise to new ideas to overcome depression.
- Go to a serene place and coolly analyze what bugs you. It will provide solutions.
- Hit gym regularly and do workout as it helps you raise your energy and enthusiasm.
- Be in the company of people who have sense of humor and enjoy their company.
- Focus more on your passionate areas and hobbies. These things would kick start your mind with positive vibrations.
- Self-hypnotism helps in overcoming depression.
- Regular open discussions by parents with their children will help free flow of ideas about the problems and prospects within the family members.
- Build bridges not barriers. Develop supporting relations at the workplace so that you can share your problems if any. It provides ventilation to your hidden emotions and feelings resulting into relaxation of your mind.

Takeaways

Remember that there is nothing stable in human affairs; therefore avoid undue elation in prosperity, or undue depression in adversity. - Socrates

No one has the right to depress you. You alone are responsible if you are depressed as you allowed your mind to get depressed. Depression is a common illness. It exists among all individuals at some point of time in their lives. The intensity varies. When it goes at peak level then it is the time to take a relook at it and take immediate corrective action. It is problematic when it goes extreme and unmanageable.

The world has become highly complex. The children should be inculcated with confidence so that they don't get into depression. They should be taught to handle the challenges of life right from childhood itself so that they will be confident to take on the challenges in their lives. They become independent as well.

Look at things positively; possess positive attitude, right attitude and strong attitude to avoid depression coming closer to you. Learn to empathize with others rather than feeling sorry for the events or blaming others. Look at the problems on a clean slate. Depression is a state of mind and everybody can overcome easily provided they accept and realize that they have depression and take remedial measures immediately. People, in general, assume that their problems are bigger than that of others. But in reality, people don't realize that others also have the problems probably bigger than them.

To sum up, past cannot be changed and future cannot be predicted. Therefore, learn to live in the present to avoid depression.

MANAGING YOUR ANGER

On the other day when Ken was role playing in a Soft Skills Workshop, a person hit his spectacles and it was broken. Suddenly he got angry and he thought of hitting the other person back. Ken could not control his feelings and emotions for a moment and he was about to burst because he did not have any spare spects at that time. But he immediately controlled his anger because it happened accidentally, unconsciously and unintentionally. The other person regretted for hitting and for breaking his spects even though it happened without any negative intention. Had the situation been intentional Ken would have suddenly expressed his anger and would have warned the offender sternly for the same.

What is Anger?

It is a state of emotional outburst related to the psyche of the individual. Some people ascribe it due to genetic factors and some are grown up to be angry when their social upbringing was subjected to severe criticism in their childhood. Also when a section of people are neglected for a long time or suppressed they vent out anger in multiple proportions. One thing is certain and sure that there is always danger in anger. A few people express anger frequently by their very nature.

Causes

Psychology of an individual plays a crucial role in finding out the reasoning for sudden outburst. The inability to judge the people properly or due to preconceived notions or prejudices can result into anger. Whenever there is a vast gap between one's expectations and realities, the problem begins. Individuals tend to develop either sympathy or antipathy towards other individuals. If there is strong antipathy against a particular person, then again the problems crop in. When the issues are kept pending or when not addressed appropriately, that becomes a danger signal. Lack of openness and sharing can create problems. It is often the clash of egos and conflicts. Wrong inputs may lead to complications. Improper time management at the work place may result in delay leading to anger. When an individual is unable to look at the things from others' perspective due to lack of empathy, then also anger builds up.

At the work front when an individual does not reach his prescribed targets then the emotions outburst and self-criticism starts. Both the internal and external factors play crucial deciding factors. An individual attacks on others if there is any external pressure.

Effects

It is like tsunami effect for both the individual and for the individuals in and around both physically and psychologically. Heart beat increases and may result in transferring the anger to somebody and which further complicates the matter. There will be no concentration on the work and leading to negativism and feeling strongly that all are wrong.

At the corporate level due to the increased competition and workload, people are developing high stress levels and subsequently burning out. Long years of relations that have been tried and tested and are built based on mutual trust and confidence will break up with in no time. In corporate world, anger results in loss of clients and business, this in turn leads to loss of prospects. Society does not accept people with anger and such people become socially inept. They are treated as liability not as an asset in the corporate world. It ends in loss of respect and image. Of course, there is sudden relief to mind and one feels relaxed after losing temper. One can recoup fresh energies, which is the only silver lining over the dark cloud of anger. 'Where there is anger, there will be affection' goes famous Tamil saying which is a positivism from negative temper.

How to Tame?

The first and foremost thing is not to attack the person but the behavior of the person. Identify the problem why the other person went that much extreme. Once the hidden feelings or emotions are noticed then the half battle on anger is won. Firstly, the angered person must label his feelings. Secondly, there is need to express and report the root cause of such feelings. Thirdly, there is a strong need to take action before it becomes a volcano. And fourthly, there is a need to follow up the entire process in a systematic manner.

An individual must introspect and take intrapersonal feedback within himself about the causes, consequences and then about the credibility of the anger. If an individual is honest at the core he can judge himself and can come out of it successfully. Secondly, he can meet a trusted friend and explain the scenario frankly in order to verify and cross check from his judgement. If there is contradiction between the individual and the other person then the solution, which is more genuine, should be adopted.

An individual can go and talk to friends forgetting the anger and relax himself. While sympathy makes the other person better it is, in fact, the empathy that makes the other person stronger. Pinpointing the problem is the right method and analyzing the same from the root provides the right solution. A mature man resorts to quick correction and limits the damage. It requires extraordinary courage to go for self-analysis and introspection to manage the damage. Doing meditation and yoga can bring fresh energies to the mind. It also enhances creative energy and brings down the tempers to the lowest level. Addressing and redressing the grievances without any delay is essential.

Anger Management

The organizations are taking the concept of anger management very seriously and the concept is added in many seminars because of growing stress levels due to stiff competition. Everyone is serious and is working harder and smarter in order to prove himself. When one fails in reaching ones targets or goals or deadlines at the work front then there will be strained relations with in the companies.

Drinking water when one feels that one is irritated and feels strongly that it will result into sudden outburst will prove to be handy. Counting numbers from 1 to 10 and vice versa can contain the anger. Keeping quiet for sometime is also a good thing. Or leave the room so that the tempers can be averted. It is also necessary to go separately from the scene and do inhaling and exhaling exercises as it avoids embarrassing situation and also gives fresh oxygen to mind. Be cool and go in front of the mirror and force yourself for a repeated smile.

Takeaways

Amitabh Bachhan was known as an angry young man in his initial celluloid career. He put his anger in aggression and acted in selective roles and succeeded in his celluloid world. He knew his strengths and weaknesses and he intelligently converted his weaknesses into strengths by channeling his energies in a creative and stylish manner.

Globally renowned Gold sportsperson, Tiger Woods is also noted for aggression and his razor sharp tongue. He also utilized his energies in a constructive and creative manner and is a global celebrity.

HOW TO MAINTAIN WORK-LIFE BALANCE?

I arise in the morning torn between the desire to improve the world and a desire to enjoy the world. This makes it hard to plan the day. — E.B.White.

Now days, every successful person undergoes a major problem in this world. That is how to manage his professional success with personal and social success and how to strike the right chord between his life and his work. Success is taking its toll. People are in the mad race to achieve everything but at their own peril. They make a lot of money and create comforts but ultimately lose their mental peace.

Four Types of People

There are four categories of people — Directors, Thinkers, Socializers and Relaters. The Directors' type of people is task oriented and directs the things to be done and is highly energetic. They care least for sentiments and are hard core doers and push ahead despite odds. They achieve a lot in their life and unfortunately at the end there will be no one to celebrate their success as they rarely socialized with others and never made friends. They always remain alone right from the beginning to the end.

The second category of the people is Thinkers. This kind of people read a lot, has an eye for detail and always thinks a lot and is of less directorial tendencies and least of socializing skills. They tend to become philosophers, great thinkers in the world. They do not like to be disturbed and are comfortable in thinking alone always about their chosen field of life.

The third category of people is Socializers and is party animals. They are less of task oriented and less of thinkers and take the roles and responsibilities lightly and think about always enjoying in groups. They like to attend parties and make friends. They always take pleasure in moving with people and partying. The Richard Branson of Virginia group, UK is a party animal. He spends considerable amount of time in attending parties. Vijay Mallya of UB group in India is also a party animal and is a media savvy. He always likes to be focused and is always at the center of attraction.

The fourth category of people is Relaters and they are less of directorial, least of thinkers, average of socializing and predominant in networking and building relations.

Every individual has all the four dimensions of a personality and the quality or trait that is predominant is categorized. This analysis will definitely help people in managing work life balance keeping their tastes and temperaments in view.

Division of 24 Hours

God gifted 24 hours a day equally for all people. How to utilize the precious time is a million dollar question. An average individual spends 8 hours for sleeping, 8 hours for work and 8 hours for other routine and regular activities. There should not be any adjustment in sleeping time as body needs rest and to get recharged for the rest of the time. People spend lot of time from commuting from residence to work place and back. If efforts are made to keep the residence as close as to the work place, the time can be saved as well as the strain and stress can be minimized. The time so saved can be utilized either towards recreation or pursuing hobbies. John Wanamaker said, "People who can't find time for recreation are obliged sooner or later to find time for illness".

Gujarati Culture

Gujaratis in India work very hard and once in a week they have the culture to dine out. They do not mix business life with personal life and they are often successful in separating the both. The chunk of entrepreneurs has come from Gujarati community. They have flair for business and work with lot of dedication, discipline and determination. But once in a week they go outside with family and spend their personal and social life. Similarly most of them take periodical holidays from the work and enjoy their life.

IT Sector in India

Information Technology (IT) sector in India is doing very good. There are more job opportunities due to the IT boom. Just after the completion of professional qualifications like B.Tech and MCA (engineering graduates and computer post graduates), the applicants are getting jobs. The pay and perks are encouraging. But the work life is highly complicated and highly demanding. There are many pulls and pressures during the work life. There are too many commitments and deadlines and there are too much of unpredictable peaks and troughs during the course of the working time. All these things make the work as a hectic activity and a strenuous one. Sitting in front the computer systems is leading to developing stiff neck problems, dry eyes, irritation, lack of interest towards sexual activities, back pains etc., It looks like having everything but losing so many things related to health and recreation.

However, there is a silver lining. The IT companies are realizing the perils of working long hours. It all looks that employees are contributing their best but when we look at qualitatively the results are poor. What is ultimately essential is the qualitative not quantitative productivity. So during the working hours itself a few companies are providing time to do meditation so that the employees can regain their lost energies and work energetically. Intermittently, breaks are provided to employees for recouping their energies. Weekend parties are conducted to take time off and to unwind and to recharge for the following working day. Periodically cultural programs are organized to make the employees happy and feel comfortable. It is at the functions the employees forget the discrimination in their ranks and cadres and also forget the differences, if any, in their work life and come under one platform in the name of cultural programs.

In the western countries and many other countries, there is 5 day week. People work very hard up to 5 days and take a weekend break and spend their personal and social life with ecstasy. We have come to the world to achieve something and to contribute something that does mean sacrificing our personal lives for the sake of professional life. No one should regret at the last leg of life for not having spent personal life meaningfully. There should not be any regrets at the end of the life either not having spent personal, social or professional life.

Tools for Better Work-Life Balance

If you are losing your leisure, look out; you may be losing your soul. — Logan P.Smith.

Efforts should be made not to mix up personal life with professional life. There should not be an encroachment. If personal life is paid more attention the professional life will get disturbed and as a result losing the job and income. On the other hand, if the professional life is paid more attention, the personal life is adversely affected resulting into higher stress levels. In this context, it is aptly said, "I have more to do than anyone else; I can't possibly do everything during the day. I often end up taking work home with me".

It is a well admitted fact that money is not everything. Money is essential for survival and for having comforts but too much emphasis on money is like losing so much for so little.

Plan and execute your tasks as per your schedule to avoid any stress. And also anticipate the probable problems that are likely to come up and may create tensions.

You must be in a position to discount any external threats that can not be expected but can be anticipated. Such things will divert the routine work thereby getting deviated. Apart from the routine tasks other tasks will pile up thereby deviating from the routine course of action resulting into stress and burn out. Internal threats can be expected and anticipated and those can be controlled and minimized easily.

Always look at the amount of investments that are put in and the probable returns that can be generated. When the returns are higher than the investments and that too when it does not affect our personal health then the work can be proceeded.

There is nothing like false prestige while undertaking the tasks as few males find it difficult to get out social stigmas like *'I can't do this'*.

Flexitime as a concept is widely applied in the corporate world. It allows the employees to work the stipulated hours either at a stretch or in a piecemeal manner.Especially when both the wife and husband are working the flextime helps in right division of work at home.

Allocate your time properly everyday for personal, professional and social life. It is necessary to strictly demarcate all the activities as per schedule and follow accordingly.

Multitasking is the buzzword at the corporate world. But it is leading to so many complications and implications. Do not have all priorities at a time.

Cut down superfluous tasks. Prioritize and plan the tasks properly.

Find out the passionate areas and activities that interest you. And pursue the same up to the hilt. Since you are enjoying what you are doing you will not get stressed out.

Achievement and enjoyment are two sides of the same coin. Try to strike the right balance between the both so as to lead a smooth, successful and comfortable life.

Cultivate positive attitude, inculcate coping skills and pursue creative hobbies and interests to maintain the right balance between the work and life.

It is desirable to hit gym or for a walk to beat regular work related stress. Pursing hobbies like swimming, games and other activities regularly relieve stress and enthuse the individual with fresh energy. Going for meditation also helps.

Research reveals that "American workers average approximately ten paid holidays per year while British workers average twenty five holidays and German employees thirty. Americans work twelve weeks more a year in total hours than Europeans". Enhancing paid holidays will help employees to be more secure financially. They can avail paid leaves and go for holidaying for unwinding. Many corporates provides paid leave once in a year with free traveling allowances to their employees.

Daily make a habit to spend a few minutes in a serene and silent place by closing your eyes. In this scenario, you neither hear anything nor do you see anything. As a result, you can immediately consolidate and create fresh energies.

Takeaways

Life is very short and let us make it sweet. Striking the right balance amongst the personal life, professional life and social life is essential. To sum up in the words of Theodore Roosevelt, "When you play, play hard; when you work, don't play at all".

HOW TO GIVE FEEDBACK?

A successful person is one who can lay a firm foundation with the bricks that others throw at him or her. - David Brinkley

What is Feedback?

"Feedback can be defined as the tool that projects and presents the information which highlights if there are any gaps between the intentions and the actions with in the individual as well as if there is any gap between the expectations and aspirations of the giver (employer) and the receiver (employee) in achieving the goals and objectives of the organization"- Prof.M.S.Rao.

Stages of Feedback

While providing feedback, dispassionately describe the behavior of the person with entire information. Convey your feelings objectively and specifically without hurting the other person. Explain the impact and the implications and complications involved in such kind of behavior. And request or implore the other person to change his intentions, actions and behavior as it will help in having better personality and command respect among all. There has to be etiquette in all the stages of feedback in order to have effectiveness.

Types

There are different types of feedback such as positive feedback, negative feedback, bipolar feedback and sandwich feedback etc,

If the end result of the feedback is in favor of the individual and that makes him/her happy and comfortable it is said to be positive feedback. On the other hand, if the outcome of the report or feedback is not palatable to the other person and requires drastic correction for improvement then it is known as negative feedback. Third method of feedback is the bipolar one which is blend of both appreciation and correction. There is a polished manner and method of giving feedback which is known as sandwich method. In this method, the negative comments are embedded between positive comments. Such as this kind of feedback starts with a positive sentence of praise followed by the intended information conveyed to be negative for correction and then quickly and smartly concluded with positive praise. For instance, *"Sangeeta, you are so sweet and cute in appearance. Unfortunately the attire is not matching to the function. Of course, your manners appeal me the most".*

Importance

Learning is a process from cradle to grave. And one can learn effectively and efficiently if the feedback is taken continuously. The feedback appraiser must be someone who is fair, dispassionate and impartial to judge, evaluate and provide constructive feedback for progress.

Constructive feedback reinforces the strengths and helps in overcoming the weaknesses and provides the direction to the areas that need to be improved.

There are appraisers in corporates who are exclusively meant for evaluating the employees for their performance. If there are any shortfalls the employee skills and abilities are upgraded by providing proper training. Human resources are the most precious capital in any organization. Feedback, as a tool, helps the organizations to measure the standards of the employees also such as Total Quality Management (TQM). In this cut throat competitive world, all organizations are stressing on human capital.

The organizations are employing specialized professionals for feedback evaluation and it indicates the growing significance towards evaluation of feedback.

Case Study of Varun

Varun was a hardworking student in an engineering college and when Varun gave negative and constructive feedback to his faculty, the latter awarded minimum marks in the internal examinations. Who was at fault? The faculty? or the student? It is certainly the faculty for not having taken the feedback constructively. There is always room for improvement and the probable areas needs to be improved. Unfortunately the faculty could not digest the negative feedback.

Case Study of Pooja

Pooja was an excellent speaker and delivered a wonderful seminar on a topic. At the end of the seminar Pooja asked her teaching faculty to give feedback. The faculty highlighted all the positive elements and ingredients such as delivery, flow, command, confidence, knowledge, relevance to the topic and she felt greatly excited. Subsequently the teaching faculty asked her to meet in his cabin. In the cabin, the faculty personally commented, *"Your speech was excellent with total command, control and confidence in communication. However there was a flaw in your body language that is keeping a leg apart while standing that looks inviting others and that needs to be improved. Rest everything was superb"*. In this context the faculty gave a positive feedback in public and a sandwich feedback in private.

Case Study of an Interview

John applied for the post of Soft Skills trainer in a Business School and was called for interview. It was a panel interview consisting of eight persons from different disciplines including Human Resources (HR) person. The interview was conducted in a professional manner and it took around 20 minutes and at the end of the interview one of the members asked John to conduct a training activity so that they could judge for his suitability and capability to the post. John was expert in conducting interviews, group discussions, team games and other practical oriented activities. The panel member asked John to conduct the group discussion for the panel members and provide feedback.

John immediately took the charge and explained the dos and don'ts to be followed and gave a controversial topic so as to make the group discussion interesting and exciting. The panel members discussed with in the given time and there were heated exchanges of views and opinions and once the stipulated time was over, John stopped and provided feedback to each individual. After listening everything they insisted John to give negative feedback such as by highlighting only the weaknesses of each panel member and John found himself in a trap. Because it is human nature to take positive feedback and negative feedback is usually resisted. That too during interview while seeking employment giving negative feedback proved to be a big risk.

But John started by saying, "You are the veterans in your own disciplines. I am not competent to comment about your competency but since you are insisting on negative feedback I will provide. I will not like to call weaknesses rather I would like to call these are the areas for improvement". And John listed out the areas for improvement on an individual basis. And at the end John said, "Over all, you panel members have done extraordinarily well by putting your effort, energy and enthusiasm and I am highly honored to provide you such feedback".

This is the case of sandwich feedback. Giving feedback requires a lot of experience, tact and diplomacy.

Tips While Giving Feedback

- Never mix up the issues with the individuals. Give importance to issues not individuals. It helps the other person to receive feedback positively and constructively.
- Be specific and objective. Elaborate the specific part of the problem and then give feedback with justification. It should be logical and analytically supported and substantiated.
- Praise in public and criticize in private. If the feedback is positive and worth to be appreciated give it in the presence of all so the person feels elevated. On the other hand, if the feedback is negative call personally to the cabin or cubicle and then offer your comments for correction.

- Don't praise for the sake of praising as it loses its touch. The other person feels that it is flattery.
- Catch up the situation and find the person doing the right things and then praise. It is the right time to pat and the person will enhance his performance also.
- Don't be selective and choosy in appreciation and praise as it develops a great good will among the appreciated people but creates greater bad will among the majority of the people. As it is known that people getting positive feedback are few in number where as the people getting negative feedback are usually more in number. To put it precisely there should not be any favoritism in giving positive feedback.
- At times the actions prove to be wrong although the intentions are good and it is the other way round like although intentions are wrong the actions seem to be positive. Often the good intentions of our best relatives prove worse than the bad intentions of our worst enemies. There has to be consistency in intentions and actions.
- Never keep praising the same individual continuously as others might view it as partiality or bias. Find out the strengths of each individual and highlight the same in the feedback.
- Avoid comparisons with other people as it leads to ego clashes and ill feelings. Remember that everybody is unique in this world. Even the twins are not alike in attitude and aptitude.
- Offer only your comments not your judgments.

Tips While Receiving Feedback

- Listen carefully to the person providing feedback. Don't try to defend yourself instantly if it happens to be negative. Take it in your stride.
- Learn to paraphrase the contents of the feedback, analyze, absorb and accept. Don't demonstrate either positive or negative body animation or facial animation.
- Accept gracefully and project positive body animation and positive facial animation. Ask if you have any clarifications. And also display your enthusiasm to learn the ways and means to correct the same.
- And finally thank the person for taking the time to provide constructive feedback.
- Remember one thing that no man is free from weaknesses in this world.

Takeaways

The intention of any feedback is not to harm, hurt or humiliate but to help in correcting the attitude and behavior of the individual for the progress of the individual as well as the institution in which he is working. Feedback is essential in every walk of life. There is a strong need and demand to innovate new tools and techniques for evaluation and feedback of the employees so that optimum utilization of the precious human resources can be expected and achieved.

Quote: *Health, happiness and success depend upon the fighting spirit of each person. The big thing is not what happens to us in life - but what we do about what happens to us.* - George Allen

KEY TERMS

- Personal branding
- Financial freedom
- Health is wealth
- Behavioural styles

- MBTI
- Mind management
- Solitude
- Failures
- Anger management
- Feedback
- Decision making
- Memory techniques
- Motivation and inspiration
- Depression
- Work-life balance

BRAINSTORMING EXERCISES

- Is personal branding essential to stand out from the pack? What initiatives do you take to build a brand for yourself?
- Everyone talks of *'health is wealth'*. How far do you go to maintain your health?
- Money is precious. How can you think out of the box to generate multiple sources of income? State the same and analyse for feasibility.
- As per MBTI which category is your personality? Take online tests to know your personality better. Pursue your passions accordingly.
- Write down your own techniques for enhancing your memory.
- Illustrate briefly the difference between motivation and inspiration.
- Write succinctly how did you cope up with your failures?
- Did you ever undergo depression? What measures did you take to overcome? Explore new ways of overcoming from depression.
- There are four categories of people Directors, Thinkers, Socializers and Relaters. Mention in which category you fall with justification.
- What do you mean by feedback? Recall when you gave feedback to others recently. What methodology did you apply?

ACTIVITIES

Out of the four behavioural styles mentioned such as Expressive style, Amiable style, Analytical style and Driver style, which one do you belong? Take feedback from your friends, relatives, teachers and your personal feedback. Find out what the majority of the people are saying about your behaviroural style. Accordingly, you choose your passions, interest for faster growth.

REFERENCES

Author's Blog: http://profmsr.blogspot.com

6

SUCCESS FOR STUDENTS

The young do not know enough to be prudent, and therefore they attempt the impossible — and achieve it, generation after generation. - Pearl S. Buck

LEARNING OBJECTIVES

After reading this chapter and doing the exercises, you should be able to:

- Relate success from the perspective of students.
- Explain effectively the relation between root and fruit.
- Execute SWOT analysis for yourself.
- Enhance your study skills.
- Comprehend the techniques of note taking.
- Write your failure resume for minimizing mistakes and maximizing success.

CHAPTER OUTLINE

1. Students and success
2. Teachers and students
3. SWOT analysis
4. Study skills for students
5. Note taking
6. How do students learn from failures?
7. Why to write a failure resume?

STUDENTS AND SUCCESS

Students need to brand themselves in today's competitive world. Only those who are different from others stand a chance to get employment opportunity during interview. They need to take stock of their strengths and weaknesses. They should look at in which way they are going to add value to the organizations. Such homework before going for interview will help in separating men from boys. Mere academic knowledge does not pay. They need to have special skills and abilities apart from their academic background. These skills will tip the scales in favor of getting placement. Students need to demonstrate their passion for learning and growing. They must display several skills like soft skills and traits like learning ability, molding ability, adaptability and flexibility during interview selection to get employment.

Take pride in how far you have come, have faith in how far you can go. - Anonymous.

TEACHERS AND STUDENTS

Every parent wants their child to be great. Every teacher wants their students to become great. Every root delivers fruit. But what is common among all these examples is that all are torchbearers and show light. They guide and glide from nowhere to somebody.

The root of a tree can not eat its fruits but it helps others in enjoying the fruits. It enjoys when someone eats its fruits and derives a great joy and happiness. Its role is to have a strong foundation so that it can sustain for longer time in providing fruits for others. In our daily life, we find a few people who remain as root but share their fruits to others and deriving immense pleasure out of it. These people remain as a source of inspiration and motivation for others to dream big and achieve greater heights.

Similarly teachers enjoy in giving out their knowledge and wisdom to students. They feel proud when their students reaching tipping point. The teachers can not reach tipping point but they encourage and educate their students reaching the same. They enjoy in shaping the career and lives of their students.

Every parent wants their children to grow and successful. They provide character and confidence in their children which are the foundation for success. They do not expect anything from their children except love and affection.

There are people who would love to share their knowledge with others as they enjoy others' growing. It is like a candle providing light for others and getting melted during the process. And there is immense pleasure in getting melted as they provide light for others as long as they are alive.

SWOT ANALYSIS

In corporate language, SWOT analysis is defined as the rational and overall evaluation of a company's strengths, weaknesses, opportunities and threats which are likely to affect the strategic choices significantly. Albert S Humphrey was the father of SWOT analysis.

Every organization, or an individual or a country can go for this analysis periodically so as to meet its objectives and goals. Corporate planner or a strategist is involved in organization to conduct this analysis more effectively and efficiently. The person must be highly competent, motivated with a positive bent of mind without any prejudices or biases. He must be in a position to work harder under stress and strain and in a mature and cool manner so as to bring out the best results from this analysis.

As the term implies, strength means the positive side of a picture, weakness means inability to possess specific trait or quality. A threat is a challenge posed due to unfavorable trend or development till a defensive mechanism is created. An opportunity means the availability of various positive options for growth. Both strengths and weaknesses fall in internal environment and opportunities and threats fall in external environment. It is relatively easy to predict the internal environment while it is difficult to anticipate external environment. Visionaries always identify opportunities from threats as the saying goes 'An optimist looks for opportunity in the difficulties while a pessimist sees difficulty in the opportunities'. For instance, late Dhirubhai H Ambani was a great visionary as he converted weaknesses into strengths and intelligently identified opportunities from threats in the era of controlled economy and built the Reliance Empire within a span of three decades.

SWOT Analysis of a Small Scale Industry

Let us take the case study of Baba Bharath Hydrofluids, a low profile company run by Chief Business Executive, Mr. Sura Hara Prasad which is located at Nemli in the district of Nizamabad of Andhra Pradesh dealing with the manufacturing and marketing of cleaning liquids.

The strength of this company is its strong presence in many districts of Telangana region in Andhra Pradesh with strong marketing network created by way of good relations, strong financial background and highly motivated and dedicated workforce.

The weakness is that, it is not able to expand further to other regions of Andhra Pradesh due to technical problems.

The opportunities are that, this particular segment has wider scope as consumers are conscious of health and hygiene factors due to growing literacy and affordability arising out of higher disposable income levels. The company can gradually look at exports as an alternative option as its products are highly qualitative.

The threats are that, being a Small Scale Industry, it is finding a great difficulty in standing up against stiff competition from big brands in this segment. And being a fast growing company, the lesser known companies can go for duplicating these products and bringing disrepute to these brands.

SWOT Analysis of an Engg. Student

Let us look at the SWOT analysis of a fresh Engg. Graduate. The qualification itself becomes a great strength. Achievement in the academic career from primary level can be listed chronologically and also any extracurricular activities like NCC, NSS, and sports. If any prizes or awards won in any college events either at the regional level or at the national level can be stated. Knowledge of any foreign language can be considered as a plus point because if the prospective employer has an office in that specific country, the candidate can be posted there for better communication and results. Publication of any conference papers on a specific subject can come in handy. If the candidate worked on part time and gained experience it will be beneficial. In addition, the organizations expect experienced candidates. Besides, if any part time courses or training, if the person had undergone along with his/her regular degree, can also become a great asset.

When listing out the weaknesses, the candidate has to be tactful and also to be honest as incorrect evaluation will prove to be counter productive. Since the graduate has passed out freshly, lack of experience is a major weakness. Now-a-days, majority of the candidates do not posses soft skills despite being strong at hard skills. A few people may not like to go on posting to specific places and it can become a major weakness. The candidate must list out honestly if any weaknesses in academic career. Else, the organizations are intelligent enough to find out the weaknesses resulting in termination of employment.

Now-a-days, the opportunities are plenty due to fast growing Indian economy. Many multinational companies are setting up offices and manufacturing units in India thus generating employment opportunities. Besides, India is very strong at Information Technology and leading in many other sectors. An average graduate can get employment very easily if he slogs hard. Companies are offering many facilities apart from regular pay and perks. The candidates even after getting placement can go for higher qualifications, courses and find ample opportunities all around and can improve financially, mentally and intellectually. Job fairs are conducted frequently in various locations in India with walk-in-interviews with their resumes and get placements instantly. The candidates who are replete with stuff and stamina need not to fear for placement and, on the other hand, get many options to pursue career of their taste and temperament. They must note that getting placement is only a comma not a full stop because they must acquire many more qualifications, competencies, skills, abilities and experience till their end and that becomes their full stop.

At times, it so happens, the candidates may not get right placement and it is worthwhile to pursue a less profile career so as to gain experience which may serve as a launching pad for better prospects elsewhere in their next move.

The slogan of today is *'perform or perish'*. One who does not perform well or does not get adjusted well, will be served with pink slips and that becomes a major threat. If the candidate joined in the organization as proper openings were not available elsewhere and if that company is not doing well, then sticking on to it can become a threat. It may also happen that the company may not find the right person for the right slot and if it subsequently finds a better and more suitable person, and then also there is a possibility of firing the existing staff.

Likewise candidates must resort to honest evaluation of their strengths, weaknesses, opportunities and threats vis-à-vis their career and must proceed with confidence and optimism. Lot of home work needs to be done before applying for post; otherwise, it will be like a round peg in a square hole or like a square peg in a round hole.

To sum up, one must reinforce ones strengths, overcome weaknesses, manage threats effectively and must explore the available opportunities up to the hilt assuming that once the opportunity is lost, it is lost forever.

STUDY SKILLS FOR STUDENTS

Reading maketh a full man; conference a ready man; and writing an exact man. - Francis Bacon

Students spend most of their time in preparing for classes, examinations and acquiring knowledge on various subjects. Many of them don't know how to put smart work. In contrast, they put in their hard work and struggle a lot to understand and grasp their academic content. They put in quantitative rather than qualitative efforts resulting into wastage of time as well as getting concerned over the results. Right study skills will help them to emerge and evolve as successful students.

What are Study Skills?

The methodology of planning and preparing for studying either in academic or non-academic activities for assimilation of the content for better analysis, application and practice can be called study skills. It is obvious that no two people study in a similar manner. Everyone has a unique way of preparation and methodology towards study skills. It is also an admitted fact that what works for one may not work for another.

Study skills are different from academic skills. While study skills are forever the academic skills are for short term. In addition, academic skills end the day academic life ends whereas the study skills end the day the life ends.

SQ3R Technique

SQ3R is the acronym for Survey, Question, Read, Recite and Review. It is a tool that helps in enhancing your study skills. According to this method, the reader has to survey the overall broad picture about the content to be studied. The reader has to question about the takeaways out of the study from the available content as it helps in focusing better. While reading it is essential to look for the key concepts and keywords from which the meaning of the entire content in a given context can be learnt. Reciting what was read will help in retaining the content for longer time. Finally, the reader has to review what was read. It is like looking and checking for takeaways. The SQ3R is an excellent method that helps in effective study skills.

Importance

The study skills help in optimum utilization of time for assimilating and absorbing the content. Every individual has unique learning style. Being strong at study skills will help in better understanding, grasping and retaining the content. It develops and promotes mental faculties. Being good at study skills promotes smart work. It promotes competitive advantages over others.

How to Hone Your Study Skills?

Some people are auditory learners as they learn well by listening. Some people are visual learners as they learn well by seeing. However, we also find people learning through interactive learning. You may find out which category of learner you are as it enables you to effective study skills. Below are the tips for honing study skills.

1. Always study in a serene place where you don't find distractions. Selection of the study place is equally important. Avoid being surrounded by people who talk negative things like gossips, rumors, criticism, and always talking ill of others. It not only diverts your mind from study but also fills with negative information.
2. Study when you have the mood to study. *i.e.,* Check your biological clock. If you are a morning man, study during morning time for better grasping.
3. Take breaks during study as it gives your brain rest. It helps in better concentration, rejuvenation, understanding and grasping of the content.
4. Don't cram. Learn to understand first rather than mugging up the content. When the content is well understood it can be presented in your own language as you know the content thoroughly since you did not cram.

5. Admit the fact is that short pencil is better than a long memory. Take notes wherever and whenever necessary.
6. Preparing the subject which is ahead of lecture will help in asking the right questions to the teacher. It also helps you to prepare yourself mentally to attend the class attentively. It enhances your listening and attentive skills in the classroom. It sends right signals to the lecturer for conducting an effective class.
7. Don't dribble away your precious time during your study. Learn to manage your time effectively and efficiently.
8. If the content is big, break it into small chunks and allot time slot for each chunk. If you find that specific chunk is difficult to understand then select your style of reading and mood at which you can learn well and allot more time to understand and assimilate. Always allocate your priority of time for the difficult portions so that you can decode the complicated content.

Takeaways

Study skills are essential for everyone including students, teachers and professionals. Parents and teachers have a crucial role to play in enhancing study skills among children. Right planning, preparation and methodology will help in understanding and retaining the content. To conclude, effective study skills not only widen and promote your intellectual faculties but also develop your personality for achieving all round success.

NOTE TAKING

Never use a sentence when you can use a phrase, or a phrase when you can use a word. -Berkeley.

What is Note Taking?

Note taking is an art and the process of writing the content in a shorthand format in an unstructured manner without losing the essence for future reference and records. Usually, the speaking rate is faster than the writing. When any lecture takes place the entire information can not be written by the listeners. Therefore, the key and important information is written succinctly in a note book. It is a skill any one can cultivate and inculcate through right application of tools and techniques. There is also software related to this, which is known as note taking software that has several advantages.

Merits

Note taking helps in absorbing and memorizing the material effectively due to the muscular movement of hand. It helps in broadening your mental faculties. It saves time and energy. It helps in bridging the gap between speaking and writing. It can be used for future references.

Dos and Don'ts during Note Taking

1. Focus on the content not on the speaker.
2. Listen attentively to the speaker.
3. Write clearly and legibly for your clarity.

4. Write the key words.
5. Write only what is required.
6. Don't write lengthy sentences.
7. Don't sit beside your colleague as you may be disturbed during note taking.
8. Don't divert your mind.

Tips

Studies on memory have shown that, without review, 47% of what a person has just learned is forgotten in the first twenty minutes and 62% is forgotten after the first day - (University of Texas at Austin). (Reference: <http://jerz.setonhill.edu/writing/academic/notes-tips.htm)

- Develop a positive mindset about the speaker and the content as it encourages you towards note taking.
- Be attentive and listen carefully to the speaker.
- Create and develop your own method of taking notes which helps to decode as and when required.
- Write on one side of the paper so that extra information, or ideas or insights can be added later on.
- Create your own shorthand style to note down the key content that is relevant.
- Pay your attention closely and keenly on the content.
- Divide the page into three columns. In the first column write down what was taught in the class in key words. In the second column, write down the same in an elaborate form after reading from the text. In the third column, write down the queries to be posed to the teacher, if any. It saves your precious time as you don't have to duplicate the content freshly in another page book. In addition, this approach aligns the entire information in depth and making the information available on a platter.
- Use different colored highlighters to accord the priority of importance.
- Research reveals that we can recall what was taught in the class within 24 hours only by 80 per cent. Therefore, jot down immediately after the class what was said if you don't find time during the class.
- By referring textbook material before being delivered you get to know idea about the topic. Secondly it will help you to jot down what is not there in the text. By this way, note taking adds value to your knowledge as you get knowledge beyond books delivered by the teacher.
- Maintain separate notebook per subject wise. It helps in organizing the things properly and also saves your time and avoiding stress arising out of searching for the content.

Takeaways

A short pencil is always better than a long memory.

Students can do well with note taking skills. It is a skill anyone can develop and hone. In schools, note taking skills should be taught as it saves time and helps in better memory retention.

Teacher should write key content and concept on the board as it helps both the teacher and students. For teacher, it helps to teach better in the next class due to the muscular movement the key facts can better be remembered. For students, it becomes easier to write and also helps in separating grain from the chaff. Therefore, brush up your note-taking skills to achieve optimum results.

HOW DO STUDENTS LEARN FROM THEIR FAILURES?

If you got it, ask yourself why and try to repeat the action. If you failed, ask yourself why and try to learn from the experience. - Dale Carnegie

Can you have omelette without breaking the eggs? Can you have success without facing failures? Of course, not. People treat failure as a stigma which is unfortunate. In fact, man learns many things from several failures and ultimately evolves as a successful person. It is basically because; man treats every failure as a learning opportunity for his progress and prosperity.

Students usually live in their reel life as long as they are in educational institutions. They will understand the real life only when they enter into employment. There are certain things students should learn while in educational institution itself as it helps them to face the challenges at the workplace squarely.

They should learn to prepare a resume about their failures. They should first list out number of failures they encountered in their lives and should write down how they overcame from failures. Did they fail in different areas? Did they fail due to their own mistakes or due to the forces arising out of external environment? The process helps in analyzing the reasons for failures and taking corrective steps. It enhances their thinking, analytical and problem solving skills. In addition, it helps them in learning certain lessons in their lives. They can fail differently but not at the same thing several times. It makes them to think in a more realistic and practical manner. The takeaways out of their failures will help them in facing the real challenges in the corporate world with more confidence and courage.

Remember the fact that everyone has their own share of failures. If there are no failures in life, it indicates that people did not risk anything in their lives. Not to have taken a risk is also a risk. Students should learn to risk and try whatever possible as they are young and energetic. They can rise even if they fail as they are filled with energy and enthusiasm.

Always remember one thing in life there are no problems but only opportunities. Every problem offers some prospects in disguise. Students should be able to spot and tap for their advantage.

Life is not a cakewalk. It is a circus with highs and lows. Students should not get elated with success and should not get dejected when faced with failures. They must be in a position to take the challenges in their stride.

To sum up, as exercise is to your body, problems are to your mind and failures are to your success.

WHY TO WRITE A FAILURE RESUME?

When I was young, I observed that nine out of 10 things I did were failures, so I did 10 times more work. - George Bernard Shaw

Robert joined in a research center as a researcher where he had to do extensive research in his passionate area of leadership and soft skills for authoring books. He found out a few triggers and authored a book. Unfortunately the book did not sail through as it lacked research depth. He was not worried but analyzed the reasons for the failure. After thorough research he came to know the real reasons for debacle and tried again and succeeded in authoring a book on leadership which became a runaway hit. Likewise, we find many people like Robert who learns from failures and stages a smart comeback.

Importance of Failures

Failure is only the opportunity to begin again, this time more wisely. - Anonymous

Failure is like a mother who teaches many lessons. As mother stands by you through thick and thin the failure always remains with you and teaches several lessons. Everyone loves to taste success but nobody loves to face failure. People treat failure as a stigma. In fact, failure is a great teacher. It reminds you constantly not to repeat mistakes whenever you take up any challenge. Initial failures are blessing in disguise as otherwise people would remain complacent without churning any valuable takeaways throughout their lives.

The former American President Abraham Lincoln underwent several trails and tribulations throughout his life. He was a self educated man. He rightly quoted, "My great concern is not whether you have failed, but whether you are content with your failure." He failed several times. He failed to establish as a businessman. He failed in his love. He had nervous breakdown. After suffering several defeats in politics he rose to the highest position in America as the first Republican President. He failed differently but he was never dejected. He learnt lessons whenever he failed and moved forward thereby becoming stronger and successful. In brief, Lincoln lost a few battles initially so as to win a war finally.

Everyone Fails

Defeat is not the worst of failures. Not to have tried is the true failure. - George Woodberry, Poet

The fact is that everyone fails in life. If anyone claims not having encountered failure probably she/he has not tried anything worth in life. We take several decisions in our lives. All decisions may not sail through smoothly. A few fall flat. It could be due to wrong decision making or could be due to the external factors which are beyond human control. Therefore, here is a failure resume which minimizes failures and maximizes successes.

What is a Failure Resume?

Failure is, in a sense, the highway to success .... - John Keats.

Everyone speaks of success resume but here is an exception where failures are focused and we can name it as a failure resume. It is a document that lists out the number of times individuals have failed in their lives with an objective of key takeaways at the end. It should list out if there are any failures in the academic area such as failed to score high marks or failed to be a school topper. It should then focus on the failures in personal life. It could be about marriage, or career, or love or other debacles in personal life. Outline the failures in professional life. For instance, the examples in this category are inability to grow in career, inability to get along with colleagues or subordinates or superiors and inability to handle key challenges. Finally make a list of failures in your social life. Precisely, any failure resume should contain four key areas such as academic, personal, professional and social life.

Once the list of failures is written in a resume format, then it is time to analyze why have you failed. You have to be impartial to make the exercise meaningful and successful. Were the failures due to dearth of your efforts or energies or due to the external forces and factors? If things went wrong due to your personal mistake it is time to pull up your socks. On the other hand, if it were due to external reasons beyond human control you don't have to regret as most of the failures are the result of the same reasons. If you find that you have failed by repeating the same mistakes it is time to change your thinking pattern and execution process. In contrast, if you failed differently, that means, you have tried worthwhile in your life and learnt lessons out of them.

Why a Failure Resume?

Success is often achieved by those who don't know that failure is inevitable. - Coco Chanel

Life is full of highs and lows. We cannot take the things for granted with growing uncertainty and complexity arising out of rapid technological changes.

A failure resume makes you more humble as it is full of tumbles in your life. It makes you to think more logically, analytically and improves your decision making skills. It makes you to empathize with others especially who failed in life. It connects you with others sympathetically thereby building good relations. It enhances your maturity levels and keeps you cool and composed whenever you are faced with failures in future.

Students and working professionals should be asked to write a resume of failures and it should be submitted to the potential recruiters. Currently few recruiters pose questions related to failures during employment interview. The same can be extended to writing a failure resume and submitting to the potential employers. *'Failure resume'* can be prepared at any stage of life. It could be during your academic life or professional life. There is no specific time for learning mistakes in life.

How to Write a Failure Resume?

Writing a failure resume is a four step process where in the first column; write down what are the major failures in your life. In the second column, mention why have you failed? In the third column, state how you have failed and finally in the fourth column outline the lessons learnt from these failures.

Takeaways

Whenever you make a mistake or get knocked down by life, don't look back at it too long. Mistakes are life's way of teaching you. Your capacity for occasional blunders is inseparable from your capacity to reach your goals. No one wins them all, and your failures, when they happen, are just part of your growth. Shake off your blunders. How will you know your limits without an occasional failure? Never quit. Your turn will come. - Og Mandino

Writing a failure resume is essential to everyone. It is a kind of intrapersonal feedback for improvement and career growth. It provides several meaningful takeaways. As organizations encourage self-appraisals after joining, they should insist on a failure resume before joining in their organizations from their potential candidates for bringing down the failure rate and broadening the success rate.

KEY TERMS

- Students
- SWOT analysis
- Note taking
- Failure resume
- Teachers
- Study skills
- Students and failures

BRAINSTORMING EXERCISES/ACTIVITIES

- What do your mean by SWOT analysis?
- Jot down your strengths and weaknesses. How will you overcome your weaknesses?
- Write down your ways and means of study skills
- Write down your academic failures and takeaways?
- What are the strengths, weaknesses, opportunities and threats for a graduate? Explore with more illustrations.
- What did you learn about study skills? How are you going to implement for getting better?
- What lessons did you learn from Lincoln's failures?
- Do you agree to cliché 'you need to lose a battle to win a war'?

REFERENCES

Author's Blog: <http://profmsr.blogspot.com/>

<http://jerz.setonhill.edu/writing/academic/notes-tips.htm>

7

CONCLUSION

I've missed more than 9,000 shots in my career. I've lost almost 300 games. 26 times I've been trusted to take the game winning shot and missed. I've failed over and over and over again in my life and that is why I succeed. — Michael Jordan

LEARNING OBJECTIVES

After reading this chapter and doing the exercises, you should be able to:

- Compare eagles with leaders.
- Understand knowledge management.
- Appreciate sharing your knowledge with others.
- Emphasize on Knowledge, Attitude, Skills and Habits (KASH) but not cash.
- Know the importance of knowledge workers.
- Reinvent yourself constantly.
- Stick to your convictions.
- Pursue your goals with passion, persistence and perseverance.
- Appreciate author's final punch **'Failure is only a comma, not a full stop'.**

CHAPTER OUTLINE

1. Be an eagle and soar like a leader
2. Knowledge management
3. Knowledge grows when shared
4. KASH is king
5. Are knowledge workers leaders in 21st century?
6. Blend your talents and skills for success
7. Reinvent yourself
8. Never give in

9. Never give up
10. Failure is only a comma not a full stop

BE AN EAGLE AND SOAR LIKE A LEADER

When we look at turtles, they have low goals and low relationship. Sharks have high goals but low relationship. Teddy bears have high relationships but unfortunately low goals. The relationship and goals for fox is medium. It is only the eagle that has high relationship and high goals. Eagle is the only one which stands distinguished from the rest of other birds because of certain unique qualities. And these can be called as leadership qualities.

Eagle is good at goal setting. It can see any object from a distance of 500 feet. The leaders know the big picture and they set their vision. The eagle is highly focused and does not get deviated from its goals. It tries various ways and means to get its meal. Once it clearly targets the same, no amount of external factors or forces stop from acquiring. So is the case of a leader.

Eagle loves challenges and undergoes changes during lifetime which is essential for leaders. Eagle loves and thrives in thunderstorms. It believes in uncertainly and is highly confident. Eagle is a risk taker as well.

Eagles think big, dream big and dare big. They never settle for less. They want the best of everything in life. So are the leaders who are passionate, dreamers, doers and pursue their vision with dogged determination.

It is a competitive world where it is not only the fittest but also the most adaptable can survive. You have to change with rapid changing times. And to be a successful leader, you must be able to learn lessons fast from your failures, quickly correct yourself and move forward aggressively without regretting and brooding over failures.

Leaders are always compared with eagles because they soar above the crowd. They know where they are going and why they are going. No amount of external disturbances prevents them reaching their goals. Therefore, be an eagle and soar like a leader.

KNOWLEDGE MANAGEMENT

Now days, knowledge management is the buzzword in the corporate world. Companies proudly talk of it. Is it related to management of knowledge or something else? Let us find out what is all about knowledge management.

According to Andersen Consulting, knowledge management (KM) is the systematic process of acquiring, creating, capturing, synthesizing, learning and using information, insights and experiences to enable performance. It converts ideas into realities. It helps in promoting the learning curve of their employees and retaining the same for the overall prosperity and progress of the organization.

KM is interwoven with information dissemination and information action. It is linked with talent management. Constant creativity and innovation are the pillars for knowledge management. These days the companies, in order to stay ahead of their counterparts competitively, they are focusing on managing and expanding their knowledge capital base. It adds value to their organizations. However, very few companies hoard their knowledge and don't believe in sharing due to the fear of their employees poached by competitors. In such a scenario the company may not encourage their employees to grow intellectually thus resulting into stagnation.

KM promotes, furthers, nurtures knowledge in the organization and ensures that the knowledge is managed with in the company even in the event of the exit of the employees. KM highlights on collective knowledge of the enterprise through collaborative teamwork, knowledge sharing and mentoring.

The companies should provide favourable organizational culture and climate to ensure that knowledge is managed effectively and efficiently. Employees should equally actively involve in the successful sharing of knowledge. At times because of competition a few employees do not share their knowledge and retain with themselves thereby denying opportunities for others to share.

It is to be appreciated that knowledge sharing is widely honoured while the knowledge hoarding is highly dishonoured. The companies should wed knowledge management wholeheartedly not only for their survival and success but also for the all round development of their precious human resources-employees. It is rightly said that knowledge grows when shared.

KNOWLEDGE GROWS WHEN SHARED

"Rivers do not drink their own water, nor do trees eat their own fruit, nor do rain clouds eat the grains reared by them. The wealth of the noble is used solely for the benefit of others?"

John Ruskin's 'Unto This Last' to read during his thirty-six hours journey from Johannesburg to Durban, in October 1904 which changed Gandhiji's life and led to the setting up of the Phoenix Settlement. After reading Ruskin's book Mahatma Gandhi said, "I could not get any sleep that night. I was determined to change my life in accordance with the ideals of the book." Ultimately it is the ideas that change anybody's life. It proves beyond doubt that ideas and ideals rule the world.

Mahatma Gandhi led India to independence through non-violence and Satyagraha. Very few people know that he took these principles from John Ruskin's book 'Unto This Last'. Mahatma was so influenced by the thoughts and writings of Ruskin that he experimented the principles for the liberation of India from colonial yoke.

Did the author ever imagine at the time of writing that his own ideas will help a country to attain independence and setting a trend for others to follow? Never, but it happened. Taking a leaf from Mahatma Gandhi, Martin Luther King and Nelson Mandela also implemented the same principles for equal rights for Blacks along with Whites in America and abolition of apartheid in South Africa and they succeeded. Mahatma Gandhi honestly admitted that these principles were not his own but read and implemented. It is for these reasons he is revered as Mahatma Gandhi across the world.

All individuals have great ideas. Few individuals only share. And very few individuals accept and experiment. Usually the credit goes to these few individuals as they accepted, tried and tested with courage and conviction. What a great satisfaction the creator of the ideas gets when his or her ideas are accepted magnanimously and tried and tested by others successfully.

Great individuals never bother who gets credit for achievements. It is just because they are great. Many people have read John Ruskin's book. But, did how many people take his great ideas into practice?

In our real life, we find few people having vast knowledge but not sharing. It does not help in any away. What happens when water stays in one place without any movement? It stinks. As there has to be flow of water movement there has to be flow of ideas and sharing of knowledge.

At any point of time, people will have similar ideas and insights. When opened up, the same can be shared resulting into generation of more ideas. This is the essence of the day.

The world is becoming complex everyday with the rapid growing technology. More and more problems are arising as a result of complexity and uncertainty. Having multiple ideas will help to tackle the problems.

This content is dedicated to those unsung heroes and heroines who share their knowledge and ideas with others with magnanimity without expecting any rewards or credit. If the author's Blog http://profmsr.blogspot.com "Where Knowledge is Wealth" becomes the torchbearer of knowledge, ideas and ideals, it gives him a sense of great satisfaction and joy.

KASH IS KING

The world makes way for the man who knows where he is going. - Ralph Waldo Emerson.

Everyone should have goals in life as goals will motivate to move in the desired direction. Goals help stay focused. Goals help us to do something on a day to day basis as we have certain objectives to achieve in our life. Goals keep you going. But how do we set goals?

"A goal properly set is half way reached", said Abraham Lincoln. Goals must be specific. For instance, we need to specify clearly so that we can follow that particular direction. Goals must be objective. In the sense, we need to be concrete at the base level so as to know why we move in that direction. Goals must be measurable. For instance, the set goals need to be fixed with duration to reach. Goals must be achievable. It means, these should not be based on daydreams but solely based on dreams. It is rightly said, 'Vision without action is a daydream and action without vision is a nightmare'. Goals must be reachable. For instance, we the citizens of India can set the goal to become the President of India but not the President of USA. Goals must be timed so that we can hope of reaching. All these goals are succinctly called as SMART goals.

Goals should not be set based on herd instinct. There should not be any parental pressure or influence of friends or relatives. On the contrary, it should be purely based on aptitude.

Goals remove all negatives thoughts as man becomes optimistic in attitude. Viktor Frankel was a Jew who was put in concentration camp and subjected to lot of hardships. He wrote the book titled 'Man Search for Meaning'. He said that people can survive for longer time if they have goals. People survive as they have unfinished agenda — goals.

Activity

Here is an exercise that can help in setting the goals more meaningfully. Close your eyes for five minutes in a serene place and think yourself how and where you would like to be after 5 or 10 years in your life. You must cover your personal life, professional life and social life. Then, just think of the fuel required to get you going towards goals and that fuel is nothing but KASH which is the acronym for Knowledge, Attitude, Skills and Habits. What kind of knowledge is essential to reach your goals? Then the attitude to develop the goals and the requisite skills and abilities is to be listed. At last what are the best practices and habits necessary to reach the goals has to be written. After having written about the KASH then you can work on towards your goals.

Once the goals are set, it is necessary to write the same as written goals are more meaningful. Read the same twice in a day before going to bed and sooner you wake up from bed. In the night, whatever is read is firmly fixed in the mind and the same is firmly confirmed as the goals are read the moment you get up from bed. When it is made as a regular habit then the goals can be nailed firmly in the mind. The subconscious mind is so powerful that it keeps you reminding you regularly and ensures that you do not go out of the track.

In life, there are two forces or factors that disturb our plans and they are internal and external factors. In case of external factors or forces, nothing is in our hands and therefore, it is meaningless to worry for the same. But there are internal factors which are very much with us and can not be taken away that are KASH. Everyone faces failure at some point of time in life but what ultimately stands by the individuals is the KASH not cash. The founder of Honda Company was literally in shambles during the Second World War. But he rose like phoenix because of KASH. KASH keeps fuelling the individuals in pursuit of goals. KASH supplements sufficient spark to ignite the passion.

In the business parlance it is frequently said that *'cash is king'* because when goods are sold on cash the risk is eliminated. People like Narayana Murthy and Dirubhai Ambani reached from nowhere to number one position not because of any cash but because of KASH. To sum it up, KASH is always KING.

ARE KNOWLEDGE WORKERS LEADERS IN 21ST CENTURY?

The most important, and indeed the truly unique, contribution of management in the 20th Century was the fifty-fold increase in the productivity of the manual worker in manufacturing. The most important contribution management needs to make in the 21st Century is similarly to increase the productivity of knowledge work and the knowledge worker. — Drucker (1999, p135)

Who is a Knowledge Worker?

This is the nature of genius, to be able to grasp the knowable even when no one else recognizes that it is present.
- Deepak Chopra

Knowledge workers are the people with specialized area of interest. They stand different from others in their knowledge, competence, skills and abilities. They define the problems unconventionally, think creatively and innovatively and follow uncharted path for finding solutions to problems. They involve in lot of research and consultancy. These people add value to the existing knowledge with modified and updated content pertaining to their specific domain. It was Peter Drucker who coined the term Knowledge Worker way back in 1959 in his book *'The landmarks of Tomorrow'*.

Characteristics of Knowledge Workers

We know now that the source of wealth is something specifically human knowledge. If we apply knowledge to tasks we already know how to do, we call it 'productivity'. If we apply knowledge to tasks that are new and different we call it 'innovation'. Only knowledge allows us to achieve these two goals. — Drucker (1992 p23)

Knowledge workers are basically passionate people whose primary aim is to achieve something big and unique. For them, money is the secondary motivational factor. They are cut above the rest and follow the road less traveled. They love challenges and changes and they love to live on edge. They have huge appetite for knowledge and always crave for creating something new. They have passion for learning and growing. In a nut shell, it is connected to their brain rather than brawn.

Knowledge workers take pride in what they do. They are passionate learners. They aim and dream big. They are different but not indifferent. They care less about others. They are highly task oriented and always strive for hitting the bulls' eye. They have global mindset. They are more loyal to their peers than to their employers. Those who hail from the background of teaching, training, consultancy, business and research can become successful knowledge workers. Their output cannot be measured easily like any other manual work. They focus on quality of work not quantity. These people demand lot of freedom and autonomy. These people have to be handled with soft skills so as to extract their hard skills.

Why Evolution of Knowledge Workers?

Making knowledge workers productive requires changes in attitude, not only on the part of the individual knowledge worker, but on the part of the whole organization. — Drucker, (1999, p156)

The industrial revolution led to the birth of middle class people. The growing services sectors in the 20th century led to the birth of knowledge workers. With the growing rapid technology, the aspirations and expectations of the people are raising rapidly. The companies are also looking at the ways and means to beat competition. Innovation and creativity is the key to stay ahead of competition. Therefore, they are focusing on specialized services and products for the benefit of customers. To do all these things, they bank on the support of knowledge workers.

Companies prefer to recruit knowledge workers as it saves their precious time, money and energy in providing training. It is like having plug and play recruits. Getting the ready made people is a boon for corporates. They don't hesitate to pay more for the specialized skills set. The costs are far lesser than what they spend on fresh recruits.

What does it Take to be a Knowledge Worker?

Knowledge workers use their intellect to convert their ideas into products, services or processes. - Miller WC, Fostering Intellectual Capital HR Focus, 1998

The world is going to be dominated by the services sectors where the role of knowledge workers plays a key role. However, it is not easy to manage them. They want more freedom and autonomy.

They could be stubborn and adamant. They should not be treated like any other employees. They are different and unique. They thrive on challenges and love to experiment on their new ideas and insights. They want more freedom that helps them to be more creative and innovative. It is very difficult to measure their performance.

Takeaways

The most valuable assets of a 20th-century company were its production equipment. The most valuable asset of a 21st-century institution, whether business or non-business, will be its knowledge workers and their productivity. — Drucker (1999, P135)

Knowledge workers are an asset for every organization. In fact, they are the leaders in this 21st century. They can share and spread their knowledge across the world for the benefit of mankind. There is also a huge potential lying untapped in this domain. It is essential to encourage and provide favourable environment for their research and consultancy.

The future belongs to knowledge workers. The world is going to be ruled by specialists who have specific and exclusive competencies and key skills and abilities. If you want to get noticed and spotted and remembered, evolving as a knowledge worker is the right solution.

BLEND YOUR TALENTS AND SKILLS FOR SUCCESS

The key that unlocks energy is desire. It's also the key to a long and interesting life. If we expect to create any drive, any real force within ourselves, we have to get excited.- Earl Nightingale

All human beings are blessed with certain unique qualities which are called as talents. These qualities are acquired from parents. Talents are inborn and are unique. Each individual is unique. On the contrary, skills are the abilities that can be acquired by way of reading, observation, practice, and training. Both talents and skills have to be blended in order to achieve the desired outcome *i.e.,* success. It is necessary to know what the inherent talents are. Knowing yourself better helps you in realizing your hidden potential. SWOT analysis, which is the acronym for strengths, weaknesses, opportunities and threats, is the tool to discover your hidden talents, skills and abilities.

People concentrate more on skills rather on talents. Talents are hidden within you. When you tap and acquired skills in tune with your talents you can achieve all round success.

REINVENT YOURSELF

In the middle of every difficulty lies opportunity. — Albert Einstein.

Stephen failed in business and was bankrupt. He moved to another place where one of his friends helped in arranging accommodation. He joined in a new place with his family. He deeply analyzed for some time for the causes of failure in business. Having good academic qualification, he joined in an educational institution as a teacher. He never regretted about his failure but learnt lessons from them and quickly moved to the next stage and reinvented himself as a teacher. That is the power of education and reinvention.

There are many people like Stephen who move on to the next position without brooding over the problems and reinvent themselves successfully. Reinvention is essential not only for individuals but also for companies to survive and succeed in the competitive world. With the rapid changes taking place across the world due to technological inventions, reinvention is the key to survival and success. The only thing constant in this world is change and it can be affected only by constantly reinventing oneself. Continuous and constant reinvention helps in coping up with changes that take place in the external environment resulting into achieving all-round success.

Learn Habits of Successful People

Don't reinvent the wheel, just realign it. — Anthony J. D'Angelo

You can have anything you want if you really want and are willing to sweat out. Nothing is impossible. Why some people achieve success in their lives is a clear indication that everyone can achieve whatever they want. Find out the path of the successful people and how they reached their goals. What made them stand apart from the rest? Find out their qualities and characteristics. Find out what are the qualities commonly connecting you with such personalities. Acquire what you do not have and follow their path without focusing too much on success. Once it is done consistently and regularly then you don't have to run behind success rather success will run behind you.

Ron's Reinvention

The only thing new is you finding out about something. Like nothing's really new, but you reinvent it for yourself and find your inner voice. — Mike Watt

Ron was laid off as a researcher and he immediately reinvented himself. It was an opportunity to renew himself and follow his dreams of teaching. He felt like it was a boon in disguise as he basically had passion for teaching and training. Many people in the organization felt upset over the sudden closure. But Ron was basically highly motivated and optimistic who always looked at the opportunities in every adversary. It took some time for him to get out of the habits of a researcher as the profession needed activities such as sitting with the computer system for long time for searching material in the internet. Besides, he was in the comfort zone for a long time. Gradually, he came out of the comfort zone and leveraged his research skills for blending with teaching and reinvented himself as a successful faculty. Ron's transformation from being a researcher to a faculty had been smooth as he was adaptable and flexible and knew the knack of taking the best out of his past experience.

Lincoln's Reinvention

Take real life examples wherein people rose from nowhere to number one position. Abraham Lincoln reinvented himself number of times. He was almost self-educated without formal school education. He was a businessperson for a brief period where he failed. He learnt lessons and reinvented as a lawyer where he was successful. Subsequently he joined in politics where he had several successive lows. But he was not dejected over his failures. He constantly reinvented himself with the changing political scenario and ultimately became the first Republican and the 16th President of America. Lincoln's success was the result of constant reinvention.

How to Reinvent Yourself ?

I constantly try to reinvent my sensibilities and my ideas. I enjoy some of the satisfaction that I get when I feel good about what I've done. But the process is quite lonely and quite painful. — Vincent Gallo

- You have to dream big and afford big.
- You need to have lot of flexibility and adaptability.
- Break your mental barriers and limits.
- Look at successful people who continuously reinvented themselves. Take them as role models as it provides you a source of inspiration and motivation.
- Be clear what you want in life. Set out your goals and get into action.
- Spend some time each morning picturing what you will be doing and it converts into reality.

- Go for regular reading as it opens your mental windows.
- Cultivate the habit of journaling daily. It not only demonstrates your perseverance but also keeps you focused.
- When you merely sit, things don't happen. Take action, then you will find how things will happen according to you.

Takeaways

People who cannot invent and reinvent themselves must be content with borrowed postures, secondhand ideas, fitting in instead of standing out. — Warren G. Bennis

In the Hindu epics, Lord Vishnu had several incarnations. All human beings should reinvent themselves with the changing times. As body changes from cradle to grave, the human mind should also reinvent accordingly. You need to mould your ideas for reinvention. Albert Einstein once defined insanity as doing the same thing and expecting different results. To get different results, you need to put in efforts differently. It again calls for continuous reinvention on your part.

Today turbulent times call for constant reinvention for companies and individuals as well. Reinvention is the mantra for success. If you don't reinvent with changing times you stand isolated. Life is short and there is no room for regrets. Life comes only once and try your level best. Don't brood over your failures. Learn lessons from them and proceed forward. Realize the universal truth that every fall has a rise. Have firm faith in yourself. Do something for others. Serve others. Help the needy. Make difference in the lives of others. Leave a mark behind.

NEVER GIVE IN

Never give in and never give up. - Hubert H. Humphrey

Character and career is something that you should not put into somebody's hands. Character should be as per your convictions. And career should be based on your passion.

A person who compromises on everything will never succeed in his life. He will not have any identity for himself. The person who sticks to his principles and convictions through thick and thin will forever be remembered in the history of mankind. And rest will remain like lay men.

Abraham Lincoln is remembered for his anti-slavery policies. Martin Luther King is remembered for his struggle for equality of blacks along with whites through his non-violence methods. Mahatma Gandhi is also remembered for fighting for independence through truth and non-violence. All these three leaders never gave in despite assassination threats and ultimately have been assassinated. Another leader, Nelson Mandela is remembered for fighting against apartheid in South Africa. He never compromised and gave in despite being jailed for many years. What made them stand apart from others is not giving in.

It is unfortunate that a few people lose so much for so little due to dearth of principles and values in their lives. Sometimes it is also due to dearth of tenacity and resilience. The initial enthusiasm of preserving principles fades away with the passage of time and the kind of experiences one undergoes during lifetime. When people are subjected to severe trials and tribulations they tend to shift their gears from principles thereby giving in. Ultimately the difference between an ordinary and extra-ordinary person is not giving in at any cost.

For instance, there is a woman by name, Susan who is packed with principles. She works in a multinational company as an HR manager. She never bows down from her principles and values. She discharges her roles and responsibilities properly without giving any chance for others to point out. She is prompt and punctual in her work. She is very firm, strong and bold. She is respected for her impeccable and intellectual integrity and honesty.

Road to Convictions

All the strength and force of man comes from his faith in things unseen. He who believes is strong; he who doubts is weak. Strong convictions precede great actions. — James Freeman Clarke

The road to convictions is not bed of roses. In contrast, it is bed of thorns. If it were easy everybody would tread the path of convictions. What is required during the journey is faith not fear. Don't have fear but have faith in your abilities and capabilities. Only when faith overtakes fear you can wholeheartedly stick to your convictions and principles. When you are pretty sure that the path you are going is good and great then this faith alone is sufficient for you to keep you on track. Lord Jesus was crucified on a cross as he did not compromise with his convictions.

Relationships

Never for the sake of peace and quiet deny your convictions. — Dag Hammarskjold

Some people compromise a lot to sustain relationships. But it is not proper. Any relationship requires a kind of *'give and take'* attitude, where there is need for flexibility to maintain relationships. People need to strike a right balance between relationships and principles. It requires extraordinary courage to balance and sustain relations with mutual dignity and self-respect.

Sometimes, for the sake of your principles, you may have to end your relations. For instance, there was a woman by name Martina who was a capable, educated and dignified. She married with a person who was equally qualified but never respected her individuality. The husband would disturb her frequently on her routine and regular work. He was against her taking up employment. He would dominate her on each and everything and never treated her on par with him. Martina bore the brunt for too long. She tried several times to persuade her husband to change his behavior. The husband came to the extent of insulting her in the presence of others and humiliated her number of occasions. Although she loved her husband she did not like the insults and humiliations. At the end, she divorced him as she did not give in from her convictions.

Core vs. Superficial Values

Never compromise with your core values and beliefs. The core values are the basic pillars and the foundation of your personality. Core values can be compared with infrastructure while the superficial values can be compared with superstructure. There should not be any compromise on these fundamental principles. However, you may compromise in some values which are superficial. It all depends on the situation and occasion where to bend and blend your superficial values. As every man changes with the changing times, there is a need to change some of our values and principles superficially for the sake of survival.

Takeaways

He who believes is strong; he who doubts is weak. Strong convictions precede great actions. — Louisa May Alcott

Don't allow yourself to be browbeaten by others. Don't yield to pressures. Hold on to your guns firmly. Be a die hard person. Face the fight and fight on to the finish. It does not matter who wins or loses at the end. But ultimately what matters are the principles and values in waging the battle.

Don't allow others to override or dictate you. It is your life and you have to take decisions. Don't become a puppet in the hands of puppeteers. The day you become a puppet you lose your independence, individuality and originality and remain like any other average individual. Giving in-charge of your life to others is like insulting yourself. Never, never and never compromise even if it involves risking ridicule and rejection. Ultimately it is not the destination but the journey in life that matters at the end.

NEVER GIVE UP

Never, never, never, never give up. — Winston Churchill

History is replete with several examples where leaders became successful by not giving up. Perseverance, persistence and passion are the unique traits of successful people.

Let us look at few examples where people were successful by perseverance. Albert Einstein was considered to be dull academically initially. But he proved to be a great success in later part of life. Charles Darwin was an average boy initially who evolved the theory which is popularly known as Darwin's theory. Walt Disney was turned down 302 times before he got financing for his dream project. Charlie Chaplin was initially rejected for his poor acting skills. Subsequently he proved to be a great actor. Henry Ford was bankrupt initially and later proved himself as a successful entrepreneur. Thomas Edison failed number of times to invent bulb. But he was successful at the end. Had all these people given up we would not have seen several inventions. And probably we would not have heard success stories about their perseverance.

The lessons that can be learnt from these great people were - it is the perseverance and persistence that pays off at the end. It is rightly said, to win a war you need to lose a battle. At times, the temporary setbacks can not be taken as permanent ones. These should be treated as learning experiences and efforts should be made to move on.

Only the people who have seen successive failures possess the quality of not giving up at any cost. Failure is one way good as it enhances and strengthens mental faculties. It teaches several lessons. It explores new ways and means to find out solutions to problems. It encourages trying different methods of reaching goals and objectives.

Love and Success

Once you take up a task be passionate to achieve it by any means. Don't let fear to take over you or overtake you. Let your faith ride fear and force you towards your cherished goals. We have witnessed several technological revolutions which are the result of persistence and perseverance. When you love a woman can you give up? If you give up it means you don't love her. Every woman likes and loves a man who perseveres. She may initially decline falling into love. But ultimately it is the perseverance that takes you to love. Similarly success does not come on platter as it requires lot of perseverance. You need to be strong in your convictions without any let up. Never losing hope, never giving in and never giving up is the key to acquire success.

There will be several stumbling blocks to possess love. So is the case with success too. When you love a woman there will be a few who would be the stumbling blocks. Few of the stumbling blocks you know and guess and few are unknown and hidden. You need to convince yourself before you love that your love is very strong and you need to possess it. There will be few people who may be jealous with your love and throw the spanner into the process. It can be seen and removed. However, there will be a few people who you do not know. It is difficult to anticipate and manage the same. Managing and handling the both known and unknown stumbling blocks lead you towards love.

Similarly when you intend to achieve success, there will be hiccups and hurdles that you need to overcome with tenacity. There will be external forces and factors that are beyond your imagination and control that damages the prospects for achieving success. Managing both internal and external factors and forces requires zeal, energy and enthusiasm. Few people just give up when the success is close to them. They do not realize the same. Let us know that fact that it is often the last key in the bunch of keys that may open the door for success. People fail to analyze and realize the same and just give up when the success is round the corner.

Takeaways

Our greatest glory is not in never falling but in rising every time we fall. — Confucius

Keep reading the biographies of successful leaders. Read the motivational and inspirational quotes regularly. All these things inject a dose of motivation regularly and sustain you towards achieving success.

Many successful people have achieved after crossing several failures. They underwent trials and tribulations that made them very strong mentally. They learnt bitter lessons in their lives. They grew out of great difficulties and challenges. Every challenge forced them more focused and committed. It brought out the best and made them like diamonds.

To conclude in the words of Jacob A. Riis, "Look at a stone cutter hammering away at his rock, perhaps a hundred times without as much as a crack showing in it. Yet at the hundred-and-first blow it will split in two, and I know it was not the last blow that did it, but all that had gone before."

FAILURE IS ONLY A COMMA, NOT A FULL STOP

Success is like a beautiful woman who may go away at any time, but failure is like a mother who will be with you forever and teaches you many lessons.

Success is the sweetest word in the world. Failure is the hardest word in the world. But both are essential for a meaningful and successful life. While failure teaches many lessons success keeps you moving forward.

Lincoln's Failures

Failure should not alienate you and success should not elevate you. — Prof.M.S.Rao

Leaders like Abraham Lincoln are an inspiration and motivation for the people who fail miserably in life. He set an excellent example in getting along with failures and became the first Republican President of America. Whenever any individual faces failures look at this American legend who faced maximum failures successively for many years. Yet he demonstrated his dogged determination and iron will to prove the world that anything and everything is possible at any age provided lessons from the failures are well learnt.

Success - By Result

Success should never be treated as an end result rather it should be treated as a by result. You need to put in efforts and energies regularly with a view of loving to do the job. When efforts are sustained and focused for a longer time, you are sure to wed success. In Mahabharata epic, Lord Krishna rightly said, 'Do your duty and don't look for results'. When you look everything from success perspective, there is bound to be frustration as you focus more on success rather on your efforts. When you focus more on efforts not on results then success is sure to touch your toes.

Move in Matrix

You need to move in a matrix. Life is all about numbers. You need to change the strategies that do not work properly. You need to align your strategies to reach your goals. In life, there are two things to be stressed upon — one is internal environment and the other is external environment. Mostly, failure is the result of the factors and forces prevailing in the external environment. When you face failure as a result of the influence of external environment you do not have to regret. When you face failure as a result of internal environment you need to take a quick look at the strategies that did not work. You need to accept the blame, change the strategies that are feasible and possible and move forward with energy and enthusiasm. If you see the big and broad picture even some of the problems arising out of external environment can be anticipated and check-mated to avoid any fiasco. But it requires a typical and extraordinary mindset crafted from rich experience.

Examine Failures

When faced with failures just think whether you failed in the same way by applying similar strategies. In that case you need to take a relook at yourself. If you failed differently there is no cause for concern because you tried to work out different strategies towards success and the same did not work out. Therefore, examine the failures critically and creatively to learn lessons and accordingly change strategies for achieving success.

Love, Success and Age

Love and success has nothing to do with age. Anyone can love at any age and anyone can succeed at any age. If you have a big heart, love can blossom regardless of age. Similarly, if there is will power, you can achieve success by turning around failure regardless of age.

Failure — A Comma, Not a Full Stop

If you say that you have not failed, that means you have never tried. If you say that you have failed that means you are mature to admit that you tried and learnt lessons. It is folly to blame the fate for all your mistakes. As a human being it is necessary to put in best of your efforts and energies unmindful of the results. Over a period of time, success does not become a by result but an end result. To conclude, failure is only a comma, not a full stop. You can turn the tide towards success with your passion.

"Making your mark on the world is hard. If it were easy, everybody would do it. But it's not. It takes patience, it takes commitment, and it comes with plenty of failure along the way. The real test is not whether you avoid this failure, because you won't. it's whether you let it harden or shame you into inaction, or whether you learn from it; whether you choose to persevere." — Barack Obama

KEY TERMS

- Eagle and leader
- Knowledge sharing
- Knowledge workers
- Habits of successful people
- Never give in
- Never give up
- Knowledge management
- KASH
- Talents and skills
- Reinvent
- Core and superficial values
- Failure is only a comma not a full stop

BRAINSTORMING EXERCISES/ACTIVITIES:

- Jot down failures in your life.
- Analyse the reasons for failure.
- What are the takeaways?
- How can you avoid repeating mistakes?
- What do you mean by KASH?
- Narrate few people you know who rose due to their KASH?
- Write briefly how you reinvent yourself
- Name a few leaders who failed miserably and bounced back.
- Discover your talents and find out what skills you would like to hone.
- Write down the habits of the successful people. Check how many you have and how many do you have to acquire. What methodology are you going to apply to acquire the habits?

REFERENCES

Author's Blog: <http://profmsr.blogspot.com/>